Earthly Paradise

GARDEN AND COURTYARD IN ISLAM

Earthly Paradise

GARDEN AND COURTYARD IN ISLAM

JONAS LEHRMAN

with 258 photographs by the author, 15 in colour, and 49 plans

UNIVERSITY OF CALIFORNIA PRESS
Berkeley and Los Angeles

To R

If there be a Paradise
on the face of the earth,
it is here, it is here, it is here!
SADI

Frontispiece 1   A central watercourse links the various terraces of Nishat Bagh, Kashmir. This is the largest of the gardens that surround Dal Lake, and consisted originally of twelve terraces, with fountains and cascades leading down to the water's edge. Behind it, the mountains form a magnificent backdrop. Tall chenars, red and gold in the autumn, flank the canal.

UNIVERSITY OF CALIFORNIA PRESS
Berkeley and Los Angeles

Library of Congress Catalog Card Number: 80-53153
ISBN: 0–520–04363–4

© 1980 Jonas Lehrman

Printed in Great Britain by BAS Printers Limited, Over Wallop, Hampshire.
Bound in Great Britain by Webb Son & Co Ltd, Glamorgan.
Colour illustrations separated by Cliché Lux S.A., La Chaux De Fonds, Switzerland, printed in Great Britain by Balding & Mansell, Wisbech.

CONTENTS

Preface

THIS BOOK aims to present a picture of the gardens and courtyards of the Islamic world, as they exist today. It is intended to serve as a general introduction to the subject. Islamic gardens and courtyards have a very special charm and attraction of their own, and the intention here is to illustrate some of the design characteristics of those that remain. Although a brief background is given, there is no intention of producing a comprehensive history. Neither is the emphasis on landscape or botany, religion or symbolism. On the other hand, if, as a result of the illustrations of gardens and courtyards contained in these pages, a greater acquaintance is made with this particular expression of Muslim culture, further study stimulated and preservation of these special places encouraged, much will have been achieved.

Some design elements and characteristics clearly span time and place. Order, space, form, texture, pattern, light and movement have no less relevance for today's architect, artist and craftsman than they did many hundreds of years ago. And since water not only figures significantly in the old gardens and courtyards of Islam, but retains today just as much appeal, its attributes and characteristics have been illustrated in detail.

This book has a visual design emphasis. For this reason the divisions adopted may seem to cut across such expected categories as gardens that surround tombs, courtyards within mosques and *medersas*, or patios in private dwellings. Some divisions must, of necessity, be arbitrary. Inevitably there is overlap between texture and pattern, or between movement and stillness. It may also be argued that material – marble, stone, planting, and water – merits a division on its own, although illustrations in this category may be found exemplifying other criteria. Yet to categorize rigidly could eventually be misleading if not meaningless.

The core of the Islamic world was in Arabia, together with Egypt, Syria and the Mesopotamian region including Iraq. Several very early mosques with courtyards still remain in this region, but largely because of climate and terrain, the Islamic garden has best survived in countries on the periphery. Courtyards are contained within a building, and are thus an integral part of the architecture that forms them; as long as the building remains, the design of the courtyard, subject to maintenance, is likely to continue unaltered. Gardens, on the other hand, often surround a palace, residence or pavilion. They live and grow, and constancy in detail is virtually impossible to retain. Trees fill out, while flowers bloom and die, their variety and position continually subject to the needs and whims of successive generations of owners and gardeners. Nonetheless, the firm basis of Islamic belief gave rise to strong concepts of design. These in turn led to an architectural composition not solely of organic material but one constructed of traditional building elements. Paths and channels, pools, terraces and pavilions remain as firm determinants of form, quite sufficient to convey to this day the image and intention of the original designer.

Slight regional differences across the Islamic world (*Dar-al-Islam*) are to be found in the design of the courtyard, whether of mosque, theological seminary

2 The fountain basin from which the Patio de los Leones at the Alhambra, Granada, derives its name. Narrow channels lead to the centre fountain, and divide the courtyard into four. The surrounding arcade is richly decorated. Built between the 13th and 15th centuries, the Alhambra is one of the most perfectly preserved ensembles of Muslim palace, garden and courtyard.

(*medersa*) or private residence, but more significant variations occur in the design of the garden, and for this reason it is the garden that has received throughout this account the greater emphasis. What is gathered here is a selection of gardens and courtyards that have survived. Existing gardens range from the 12th to the 19th century but we know from literary and archaeological sources that gardens exhibiting Islamic influence began in the 8th century. Many have vanished over the course of time. Some have fallen into disuse, while others have been deliberately destroyed. Unfortunately, the process is continuing. Yet in spite of such adversity, the gardens and courtyards of Islam represent an aspect of culture most easily appreciated by the outside world. Unlike the European garden, which is intended for promenading, the Islamic garden is one in which to sit, to contemplate and take delight. These attractions have been maintained over many centuries, and are appreciated by Muslim and non-Muslim alike. Thus there seems sufficient justification for a focus on the design qualities of a particular aspect of Islamic culture that is not as familiar, nor necessarily as apparent as other artistic facets, such as buildings, decoration, miniatures or calligraphy.

First and foremost, the Islamic garden or courtyard is to be enjoyed. From this enjoyment may spring appreciation, and then discernment. An acquaintance with Islamic history could possibly follow, with a subsequent interest in the symbolic aspects of design, in themselves a reflection of Islamic philosophy. But for those who are prepared to use their eyes, the most appropriate comment may be given in the words of Brancusi, from the catalogue to his New York exhibition of 1933: 'Don't look for formulas – mystic or obscure. I give you pure joy. Behold my works as that which you see.'

Colour plates

I   The Emperor Babur supervises the laying out of a garden, in a later Mughal painting. Here, in miniature, are all the elements of the Islamic garden – the enclosing wall, the division into four, the cascade, the square tank and the planting with flowers and shrubs.

II   View down the Patio de la Acequia towards the north pavilion of the Generalife at Granada.

III   View, typical of many, into the courtyard of a private dwelling in Cordova.

IV   A portion of the central canal and pools in the garden of the Narenjestan-i Qavam at Shiraz.

8

Introduction

ISLAM, FROM THE ARABIC 'surrender to God', was a vision revealed to Mohammed in the 7th century; it was, and still is, also a way of life absorbed and followed by peoples of many disparate backgrounds. There was One God, Allah, and Mohammed was His Prophet. Life was ephemeral and to be enjoyed, but with abstemiousness, cleanliness and regular prayer. Muslim philosophy was wide ranging, and studies included medicine, agriculture, alchemy, astronomy, mathematics and zoology. A tenet of this religion was the unity of the diversity of experience, and this was expressed as a theme that ran through Islamic art. Geometry, ubiquitous arabesques and the rhythms within them, provided a means of symbolizing such unity.

The life led by Mohammed and his early followers was simple, and so were their buildings. The founder's dwelling was possibly roofed with branches and earth, supported by columns of palm trunks; prayers were recited under this roof and in the courtyard. But after some time a favourable comparison with the surrounding pagan temples and Christian churches was desired. A basic mosque plan, with courtyard (*sahn*), surrounding colonnade and sheltered audience or prayer hall facing Mecca, and owing not a little to the founder's way of life and manner of teaching, was subsequently established, and soon spread through areas of Islamic influence in the Middle East and North Africa.

Mosques were the sites of gatherings for prayer, although this obligation could also be fulfilled at home, at place of work or in the open air. A sermon was delivered in the larger mosques every Friday. Religious education was carried out in the mosque, which also occasionally served as a hostel for visiting scholars, and as a place of refuge against attack. The mosque served as a focus for the community. In the centre of the courtyard was a fountain and pool for ablution. The prayer hall contained a prayer niche (*mihrab*) and to the right of the niche there was sometimes a pulpit (*minbar*) often elaborately ornamented.

The *medersa* or *madrassa* was developed in Iran and the Maghrib as a theological college. Similar in plan to the mosque, it had a central court, defined sometimes on all four sides by a large portal or *iwan*, and was flanked by dormitories on one or more floors. In the mosque itself, the *iwan* was the audience or prayer hall, later accentuated by a dome behind. The form of the minaret varied widely from region to region, but it normally had a square base, which sometimes supported a cylindrical shaft and contained an inner staircase or ramp. Additional minarets were added for symmetry; they acted as a foil to the volume of the domes, and the height of both frequently rose above the city skyline. The official purpose of the minaret was to call the faithful to prayer, but it also stood as a symbol for the faith.

Early residences for the Umayyad rulers in both the Middle East and southern Spain were walled, with a single entrance leading to a courtyard surrounded by reception rooms and living quarters. Palaces often adjoined a mosque, and also shared the pattern of courtyard, audience hall, offices and private accommodation; these quarters also often contained inner gardens.

3   The dome and minarets of the Mader-i Shah Medersa at Isfahan, Iran. Basically similar to, but richer than, other Safavid mosques, the tiled dome bears a characteristic design of arabesques and stylized flowers set over a frieze of white lettering on a blue ground.

4   Windows of the upper-level students' rooms facing the courtyard of the Bou Inaniye Medersa at Meknès, Morocco. The fine stucco work, carved into both calligraphic and flowing, organic patterns, and the elaborately carved dark wood are typical of buildings in the Moorish tradition.

Facing page
5   An early morning view of the Taj Mahal at Agra, seen from the entrance gateway. This supreme achievement of Islamic architecture owes not a little to its garden setting. The mausoleum is placed at the end of the vista, on a terrace overlooking the Jumna River.

6 A richly carved doorway in the Alhambra, Granada. Interweaving geometric bands explore the subtleties possible on a flat plane, while the spaces in between have further abstract and foliated patterns.

7 Wall detail from the Alhambra, Granada, illustrating the geometric pattern of coloured tilework, as well as calligraphy and interweaving plant motifs in carved stucco. The same patterns are repeated in a variety of materials.

8 A carved stone basin in the courtyard of the Masjid-i Jami in Isfahan. The use of calligraphic decoration, usually quotations from the Quran, is universal throughout the Islamic world.

9 The two-storey arcade surrounding the courtyard of the Masjid-i Jami in Isfahan, seen reflected in the dark still water of a lobed pool typically filled to the brim. The present building on the site of an earlier mosque was begun in the 12th century, and subsequently embellished and enlarged. The tilework of the walls and galleries of the courtyard was possibly begun in the 15th century and was completed by the Safavids.

In fact, courtyards were common to dwellings throughout most of the Islamic world, owing as much to earlier living traditions and climate as to any specifically Muslim requirements. On a much larger scale were the *caravanserais* or caravan hostels for merchants and their goods, their servants and animals; these were often placed round a courtyard, and with *iwans* and oratories were in plan similar to that of the *medersa*. Courtyards were also located off the main arteries of bazaars, for which they provided fresh air, sunlight and a little quiet removed from the commercial activity.

Islamic art was freely applied to both spiritual and secular objects, and no distinction was made between these two spheres. The form of the mosque was religious, but the few objects it contained could also be found in private houses, and the tiles on its walls could be matched on secular buildings. The location and design of a pool in a *medersa* would be similar to that found in a private patio; and the geometrical layout of a garden designed for pleasure would be maintained when it later received a mausoleum.

All the Islamic arts are closely related, and reflect a common cultural inspiration. Rational abstraction expresses the significance of timelessness and this is perceptible in philosophy and mathematics as well as in architecture and the design of its attendant courtyards and gardens. A strongly marked sense of rhythm is present in Islamic architecture as well as in poetry and music; and in all such modes of expression there are endlessly repeated and elaborate decorative patterns. For example, flowers and foliage appear not only in gardens, but on domes and minarets, book covers, carpets and embroideries, and paintings.

21

12 Multicoloured faience dado on a wall of the Tomb of Moulay Ismail, Meknès. Although the theme is a flower-burst, the pattern is carried out in a strictly abstract and carefully detailed manner.

Facing page

10 A detail of inlay work of semi-precious stone set in marble in the walls of the Tomb of Itimad-ud-Daula in Agra. Every surface of the building is covered with this technique, the patterns being either geometrical, as seen here, or naturalistic.

11 Coloured glazed tilework at the Alcazar, Seville. The interweaving bands forming a geometric star pattern are perhaps the commonest of all Islamic motifs.

A prime purpose of Islamic pattern is to transform matter so that it loses its solidity or heaviness. The abstract nature of design is more significant than the material aspect, and decoration reflecting this is applied in countless ways. Walls, vaults, and floors carry deep grooves, woven patterns, sunbursts and star clusters. Undifferentiated wall surfaces are broken into proportionately related areas, rendering them more comprehensible. Regular grids are often hidden by an overlay of pattern, and often these in turn reflect further complex grids as sub-nets. Together they heighten and complement one another. Ambiguity is then created, the viewer's attention is held longer, and his sense of structure, or desire for ordering, is extended. Contemplation is encouraged and the boundary between one material and another is bridged. Ambiguity and illusion extend to infinity, and the surface is seemingly dissolved. Yet throughout the entire organization, even the smallest units are related by the overriding discipline of the geometry.

In architecture, decoration, both interior and exterior, covers a large part of the building's surface, and is related less to its structure than to its mass and proportion. For example, the transition between the dome and its square base support is made by means of small niches, further elaborated into honeycomb or stalactite (*muqarna*) work. The result is to mask the structural transition. It is a technique employed in domes, portals and prayer niches, in stone, wood, brick and faience, across the Islamic world.

23

13 Tombs of the Saadian Rulers at
Marrakesh, Morocco. Richly worked, they
are set in multicoloured tiled floors, and
surrounded by faience dados, bands of
calligraphy in both tile and carved stucco,
plant-form patterns in the same material and
stalactite archways.

Elaborate patterns in stucco and brickwork were followed by the
development of faience mosaic, in a rich variety of geometric designs. In Iran,
this led eventually to more complex curvilinear patterns in a wide range of
colours. Under the Timurids and Safavids, arabesques, floral patterns,
medallions and friezes in faience mosaic flowed over the surface of domes,
vaults, *iwans* and minarets in a manner comparable to those found in
manuscripts, carpets and metalwork. For speed of application and con-
venience, but with a slight loss of quality, faience mosaic with shape related
directly to pattern gave place to square tiles in the 15th and 16th centuries,
although the designs employed remained similar. Internally, the theme of a
rich wall surface was often expressed by a ceramic dado, over which was found
wood panelling with cupboards, or a stucco encrustation broken into niches of
varying shape for the storage of small jars, containers and other artefacts.

Possibly due to the nomadic heritage of the founders of Islam, large furniture is virtually absent from the Islamic interior. Cushions or rugs are placed on the floor, and the floor itself becomes a focus for decoration. Flagstone is a common material and stone inlay or mosaic with geometrical pattern is often used both indoors and out. Courtyards, terraces and paths often have richly textured and patterned surfaces of brick, stone or marble. Rug patterns incorporate a central element, such as a medallion, against a patterned background, or consist of an overall repetition of the same motif. The same type of pattern often radiates from a central fountain basin. Ceilings, if flat, are often richly coffered and painted, or if there is a dome, its drum may be pierced by an elaborate grillework to permit the entry of light.

The development of handicrafts took place through the evolution of techniques and continuous refinement, yet no matter how complex the pattern by which a three-dimensional object was enriched, its function was always clearly discernible. For example, an ornately carved water chute (*chadar*), beautiful in its own right, is quite clearly designed to carry out the purpose for which it was intended. The occasional injunction against a specific material (such as gold or silver), or tradition that discouraged a particular motif (such as human representation), did not inhibit the Islamic artist or craftsman, but only served to encourage his imagination.

14   Finely carved fountain basin of white marble in the *hammam* (baths) of the Emperor's private apartments at the Red Fort in Delhi. Inlay of multicoloured stone may be seen on the wall behind.

15   Water at Shalamar Bagh, Lahore, once flowed down the carved marble chute, across the shallow pool and under the Emperor's platform at the lower left. Spray from the fountain also moistened and cooled the air.

16 A late 16th-century miniature of the Feast of the Birth of Humayun shows a contemporary garden actually being used and enjoyed. In the centre is a marble-lined pool with fountain, from which water flows by way of channels on each side. The Emperor sits feasting at the back; round the fountain musicians and dancers perform, while in the foreground servants bring more food.

17 An 18th-century garden in Bengal. The formal elements are even stronger than in the last example: the long terrace, the marble balustrades, the straight canal with regular fountains and the meticulously rectangular flower beds separated by paths.

Carpets are used extensively throughout the Islamic world, and their design often portays a series of slender foliate arabesques superimposed on a pattern of infinite complexity. A major theme is the garden, or Quranic paradise, reflected by stylized flowering plants. Gardens also appear on miniatures, but generally in the form of illustrations for manuscripts and memoirs rather than in technical treatises. Frequently the subject is the ruler, surrounded by his attendants and dining or discoursing in a garden. The image is stylized, and may be somewhat removed from reality. Yet these scenes serve to show how the royal gardens were used, as well as the details they contained. Trees, flowers and streams are portrayed with carefully delineated pavilions, terraces and balustrades; and water is always present, whether static in pools, shooting into the air in fountains, tumbling down chutes or flowing through canals.

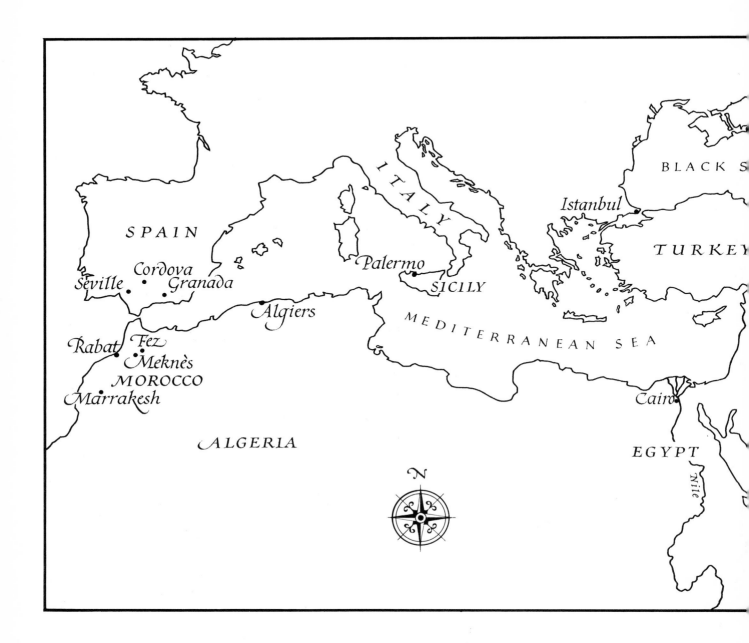

Map of the Islamic world, showing the sites of principal surviving gardens.

Setting the scene

Significance of
the garden

GARDENS, AS PART OF THE broader context of landscape design, reflect a particular relationship between man and nature. The biological and physiological aspects of man could be said to form part of the natural universe, but on the other hand, technological achievements may sometimes encourage a feeling of being above and beyond nature, with power to reorder it. When man and nature are in contact, harmony may prevail; on other occasions, there seems to be conflict. Gardens, composed of both natural and man-made elements, mirror these opposing attitudes.

A garden possibly fulfils a subconscious need for contact with something deeper than the clamouring urban world. It is a place of retreat from daily tasks and worries. It reflects harmony, and is a delight to the eye. The design of a garden is a form of art, and so echoes a particular culture, philosophy and period. On a higher plane, and in the Islamic world, it is a foretaste of paradise.

The Islamic garden performs many functions. Whether under customary private ownership or for occasional public use, it is enclosed and protected, and affords privacy. Throughout most of the Islamic world it offers relief from the stress of intense heat, while its beauty enhances the quality of living. Terraces, canals and tanks meet the demands of horticulture and irrigation, while the water also serves a desire for display and sound. Fruit trees shade planting on the ground, while flowers provide fragrance and colour.

The courtyard provides a private, protected space, symbolizing the inner life of the individual. In practice it supplies light and cool air to the rooms that form it. Even the simplest courtyard often contains a potted aromatic or flowering plant. Fountain, pool, shade and occasional tree are also a symbolic reflection of paradise.

The English word 'paradise' is derived from *pairidaeza* meaning an 'enclosure' or 'park' in old Avestan, a language that predated Persian. The Greek word *paradeisos* was adapted from the Persian, and came eventually to refer not only to the sublimity of the Persian garden but to the supreme bliss of Eden or the reward of the faithful as promised in the Quran. This Paradise was conceived as the ideal garden, and was portrayed as a state of blessedness. The description in the Quran is vivid but not detailed. Reference is made to many branches, 'spreading shade', unfailing 'fruits and fountains and pomegranates', 'fountains of running water' and 'cool pavilions'. For the believer there will also be 'couches lined with brocade', attendant houris, 'garments of silk and brocade' and 'bracelets of gold'. 'Give the message to them that believe and do good,' says the Quran, 'that they will inherit gardens through which water will flow . . . But [for] those who believe and do deeds of righteousness,' says the Quran elsewhere, 'the Gardens of Paradise shall be their hospitality, therein to dwell forever, desiring no removal of them.'

With little mention of flowers, this is a paradise based on the oasis of a desert people. The rewards reflect royalty, richness and ease; the garden is eternal, its dimensions likened to those of the sky and the earth; neither withering heat nor winter cold has any place. As Islam grew and its arts developed, an objective

18 To reach the Vale of Kashmir, where they had their gardens, the Mughal Emperors had to penetrate narrow mountain passes that made the fertile valley seem all the more luxuriant by contrast. This point on the route is at Gulmarg.

31

19 Landscape glimpsed through a row of tall trees – an effect like that of an Islamic stone or wooden screen, here reflected in the still waters of Dal Lake, Kashmir. The thin strip of land was artificially built for the purpose.

was to make the garden as close to the Quranic description as possible, and a prized garden was always compared to paradise.

D. N. Wilber recounts:

Toiling up the long, dusty road from Baghdad to Teheran in the scalding heat of summer I soon learned to seek shelter in gardens along the way, sometimes alongside a teahouse pool, banked around with potted plants, and sometimes along a rushing rivulet within a fragrant orchard. Almost at once the identification of the garden with paradise, made by the Persians, seemed natural and appropriate.

Wherever conditions permitted, gardens were established throughout the Islamic world, and were to be found in southern Spain, throughout North Africa and the Levant, and on through Iran, Afghanistan and India. Their attraction was threefold. First was the idea of Paradise as a reward for the faithful, based on many references to the Paradise Garden in the Quran. Second was the secular tradition of the royal pleasure garden, especially in Iran, a tradition which long predated the Islamic era. These two attitudes interacted with each other. Third was the particular response to the demands of terrain and climate in this part of the world, with its predominant dryness and heat. With the image of the desert oasis in mind, the creation of a formal garden, irrigated and sheltered from the outside world, provided a manifest source of delight.

The establishment of a garden meant an opportunity to reveal the essence of a site. Every locality was unique, and so to an extent were its trees and plants. The Islamic layout, customarily geometrical, only further served to express the *genius loci*, and was far from being arbitrarily imposed. By providing a cypress to punctuate the skyline, by enabling light to reflect off a pool, or by allowing the scent of jasmine and rose to fill the air, the original site was rendered more beautiful.

In Islamic literature, both poetry and prose, the garden is lavishly praised, generally by hyperbolic eulogy rather than by specific description. Earthly and sensual imagery is combined with abstract and mystical symbolism. The relationship among the garden, human life and the soul is extensively described. Garden imagery is also used to portray the beloved, and a fine balance is maintained throughout between the real and the ideal.

Although they were usually for private use, gardens were appreciated not only by members of the court and other privileged elements of society, but by all urban dwellers, whether public servants or merchants from the souk, or market-place. Gardens and also courtyards were intended to be enjoyed, and were often designed by a local ruler to encourage pleasure. Lovers delighted in the solitude and the unhappy found comfort; yet gardens could also offer a locale where nobles and the wealthy could entertain their guests with great hospitality. An owner would rarely walk through his garden, but would prefer to sit on cushions and rugs. In his pavilion, he could sit and contemplate for hours. He would observe the trees and flowers, taste the fruit and savour the fragrance; and he would listen to the birdsong, the rustle of the leaves, and the splash of water, while enjoying the garden's shade and cool air in an atmosphere of perfect peace.

20   A tiered fountain in the gardens of Topkapi Saray in Istanbul. Although its carving is of relatively late date, this fountain with its basins and pool, together with several others set amidst rich vegetation, preserves an idea of the delight yielded by the gardens at the time of the sultans.

The complementary nature of garden and courtyard

The Islamic garden and courtyard share many characteristics and balance each other. Both reflect a profound sense of place. The garden, as we have seen, expresses the concept of paradise, and is often symbolically divided into four parts. Composed of a large green area usually surrounding a centrally located palace or pavilion, it stands in complete contrast to the courtyard, which is normally within a dwelling, palace, fort, mosque or *medersa*, and bounded by an arcade. Courtyards are usually square, or nearly so, and symbolize stability; gardens are also square or at least rectangular, and when on sloping ground are terraced.

There are trees and flowers in a garden, and sometimes grass, whereas the surface of a courtyard is predominantly hard: usually stone, marble, or mosaic, although grass and trees are not excluded. But both soft vegetation and hard building material are significantly balanced by water. In a garden, water is contained in tanks, and its shape determined by channels, chutes and fountains; in a courtyard there is more restraint, and water is contained in a pool or trickled from a fountain. In fact, by its confined nature the courtyard is a feasible urban form, often small and unpretentious, lending itself to high density. The size of a garden, on the other hand, renders it less suitable for location within a city, and it is therefore usually established on the outskirts, often related to palaces and mansions, and in India to mausolea.

21, 22 A view and detail of the courtyard of a house incorporated in the Convent of Sta Catalina de Zafra in Granada. Although built in the early 16th century, the fountain and basin show how the Moorish way of life continued after the Christian conquest.

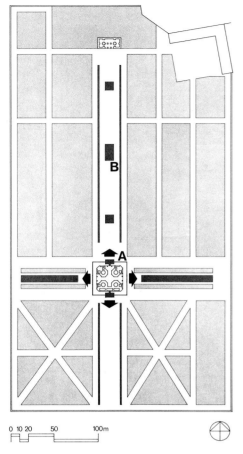

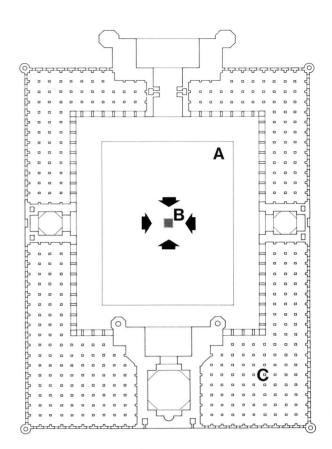

Plans 1, 2   The contrast between the outer-
directed garden and the inner-directed
courtyard is exemplified in these two plans,
one from Iran, the other from Uzbekistan.
Above: Hasht Behesht, Isfahan. The natural
movement is outward from the pavilion (A)
along the linear canals (B) to the perimeter.
The garden occupies the four corners.
Right: the Bibi Khanum Mosque,
Samarkand. Here the courtyard (A) with the
ablution fountain (B) at its centre is cut off
from the outside world by the surrounding
mosque (C) and concentrated inwards.

The main directional view designed to be taken by the occupant of a garden
is from the central edifice outward; the second most important view is from the
garden's entry towards the central edifice. In a courtyard, focus is invariably
from the peripheral arcade to the centrally located pool or fountain. The
courtyard is viewed and appreciated from its surrounding arcade, whereas
people sit within the garden itself, or in a centrally located pavilion, in order to
enjoy it.

Both garden and courtyard, when of a substantial nature, had to be designed
by architects with knowledge sufficient to provide for the water supply;
sometimes the role of designer was taken by the ruler, nobleman, or wealthy
merchant himself, who possessed not only the financial resources but also the
culture and aptitude to create the work of art which he desired to leave to
posterity.

The joy of water

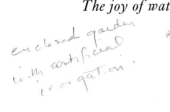

The enclosed type of garden with artificial irrigation existed in the Middle East
and Iran long before it was adopted by the Arabs and spread through the
Muslim world. The verdant symbolic kingdom or oasis sheltered from the
outside world was a very early concept. It is known that Cyrus the Younger
planted trees in straight lines to facilitate irrigation in his own paradise garden
at Sardis, and that the Sassanid palaces were surrounded by water and
vegetation. The cultures of ancient Greece, Rome and Byzantium were
influenced by the early Iranian garden tradition, which in its turn could well

35

23 A covered octagonal ablution basin in the centre of the majestically scaled courtyard of the Sultan Hassan Mosque in Cairo. The structure is largely of stone and stucco, while the courtyard paving is elaborately patterned in stone and marble.

24 A fluted stone ablution basin framed in an archway to the courtyard of the Masjid-i Hakim in Isfahan. The mosque was founded in the 12th century, and, with its arcaded courtyard of brick and tile and its central rectangular basin, provides a fine example of a mosque in this region.

Baghdad mid 8ᵗ 13ᵗ c.

have been affected by the gardens of Mesopotamia. In the Samarra of the Abbasid era, the 9th-century palace contained *iwans*, encircling walls, canals, pools and fountains, all within a formal framework of esplanades and courtyards.

Water was rich in symbolism. It was a source of life, and in a harsh landscape refreshed both body and spirit. To the Muslim, the water that maintained his city represented both its material economy and spiritual force; at the personal level, its fluidity and purity made it an image of the soul. So in gardens and courtyards water formed the symbolic centre, the basis of design. Dividing the garden into formal sections, water flowed through narrow channels, implying as it did so the passage of time – as distinct from the sea, which suggested timelessness.

Water, used for ablutions, was the symbol of purity and was found in tanks in the courtyards of mosques or *medersas*. And since paradise overflowed with water, water in these tanks always reached the brim; this required an overflow channel, which in turn formed part of the overall design. Symbolically, a cube or rectangle reflected stability or earthly paradise, and the placement of a rectangular pool on the centre axis of the garden or courtyard logically followed.

The choice of site, not only for palaces and gardens but for cities themselves, depended primarily on the availability of water. Stemming from the mountains, or from a wadi or an artificial reservoir, water would be led through an open or underground canal, aqueduct, or clay pipe to tanks or cisterns. In small settlements, the mosque often provided the only water supply. Generally, however, people carried their water from public fountains which were often set into the outer wall of a building. These would be fed from storage tanks, which in turn would be supplied from the main cistern. The wealthy had storage cisterns in their basements, and the water was then lifted to high storage tanks to feed their private fountains. Within the courtyard or garden, channels of clay, stone, or, occasionally, marble distributed water to

Water = the soul = the passage of time purity   *cube = stability or earthly paradise*

25 The central fountain in the Patio de los Leones at the Alhambra, Granada. The lions were possibly carved in the 11th century; the basin, probably three centuries later, and originally from elsewhere, carries a long poetic description attributed to Ibn Zamrak. Water basins were quite commonly supported by animals.

26 A stone basin at the entrance to the garden of the Pars Museum in Shiraz. Originally from the Masjid-i Atiq, this basin was once finely carved, but the calligraphy which covers much of its surface has weathered considerably.

27 A fountain basin set barely above the level of the paving, connected by a short channel to a deeper pool: detail of the garden of Alcazar at Cordova. This play with contrasting levels of water, creating contrasting effects of light, is among the most intriguing subtleties of Islamic garden design.

the flower beds. On flat terrain, the water courses divided the garden into four by radiating from a central pool. Apart from early symbolism, the form of the Islamic garden was determined to a large degree by the irrigation technique. Without water and shade, everything succumbed to the scorching heat.

Water was used creatively to contribute to architecture and landscape. It offered the qualities of tranquillity and depth, coolness and moisture. Pools sometimes contain fish or ducks, and encourage the growth of plants. Tanks and channels contain fountains, possibly introduced originally to clear insects from the surface of the water, but soon found to delight the eyes and ears. The falling spray generates ever-expanding ripples. 'Look at the water and look at the basin,' runs an inscription on one of the Alhambra's fountains, 'and you will not be able to tell if it is the water that is motionless or the marble which ripples.' In fact, water is an element that provides a welcome contrast to the solidity and stability of the architecture. Fountains, cascades, channels and brimming pools cool and moisten the dry air, and add an extra dimension of scintillating movement, sound and light to the courtyard and garden environment. When falling, it can provide a continuous background of sound, masking outside traffic noise, or when placid, dense silence. It can produce an effective physical and visual two-dimensional barrier, both horizontally and vertically. It can slide like a sheet of curved glass over the edge of a waterfall. The shape of this edge – smooth, serrated, curled or notched – then determines the shape of the water, and whether it is to fall free, or run back. Thus water affects the quality of the environment, supplies movement, grandeur, exuberance, sparkle and delight, and can be seen, heard and felt.

In a garden or courtyard fountain, the shape taken by the water depends on its velocity and on the shape of the nozzle. After it leaves the opening it becomes more free, subject only to friction and gravity, and held together by surface tension. Forced through tiny holes, it becomes a mist. Alternatively it rises gracefully as a thin vertical line or as a plume, fan or mushroom. Not surprisingly, its fascination is universal. Islamic fountain bases were often

28 A carved marble basin set in an octagonal recess in the paving of a courtyard in the Alcazar, Seville, the geometrical balance given life by the moving shadow. A more general view of the courtyard may be seen in plate 125.

29 Fountain basin in a courtyard outside the Gayer Anderson Museum in Cairo, a complex composition of curvilinear and straight forms. This museum, containing several Islamic artefacts, is adjacent to the Ibn Tulun Mosque.

30 Fountain-heads of white marble in a
pool on one of the two terraces that flank the
Taj Mahal at Agra. The main purpose of
these pools was to reflect the Taj, but with
their curiously lobed corners they have their
own geometrical interest.

carved, and in Mughal India sometimes contained inlay work. Even a fountain
basin was often carved to symbolize swirls of water, or, as at the Red Fort in
Delhi, an open lotus.

The water's edge is the most attractive area in an Islamic garden and so
provision for access and a hard-surfaced edge that parallels the channels is
customary. The sides of pools, however, often extend above the surrounding
ground level, and are given elaborately carved edges. Since water is scarce,
pools are shallow, but when the water is deliberately left murky, its depth
seems infinite. The reflection of the sky on the still surface of a pool introduces
light, brightness and a further impression of space, while the image of the
passing clouds symbolizes transience.

Water invites approach, remains of continuing and absorbing interest and
throughout the Islamic world has been treated with consummate skill. It has
been made straight edged, runs in marble channels, fills baths and fishponds,
flows over waterfalls, speeds down chutes and sprays the air from fountains. It
can also be still, when the flat surface of a pool is strewn with rose petals, or
when at night it bears candles set adrift on tiny rafts. Throughout most of the
Islamic world, water remains scarce; but in every garden and courtyard it is
unmistakably the focus of attention, a profound satisfaction, and a supreme
delight.

Characteristics

Order THE ACHIEVEMENT OF A universal order that symbolized the unity of God and that in practice was based on abstract principles appealed to the Islamic artist. Such a concept applied to all aspects of creative work, whether related to the design of a building, a garden, a courtyard, a carpet, or a miniature. The result was always complete, an identifiable organization with all elements related to each other.

In Islam, mathematics is the language of the intellect and its abstraction reflects the Divine Order. Man and nature are both created by God; mathematics links the structure of both and helps to explain their proportions. Shapes created by both men and nature can also be seen to share a common mathematical base. In such circumstances, geometry, symmetry, shape, surface and even line all reflect a natural process, an inherent organization. Proportion also plays a role in this process, and helps to relate the Muslim to the cosmic order.

The search for order, inherent yet perhaps not always conscious, invariably led the Muslim artist to aim for clarity and legibility, and so to the use of geometry. Based on geometry, a design might be divided and subdivided, but will still possess a unity and quality of its own that is more than the sum of its constituent parts. The system of measurement itself, involving finger, palm, foot and cubit, is based on man, and thus enables him to define spaces and to relate them to his own body. One result is a constant awareness of the human scale; another is the achievement of harmonious proportions. So while the elaborations of geometry attract the intellect and encourage further contemplation of the Divine, they also assist in the design of buildings and are the chief means by which order prevails in the Islamic garden.

The purity and perfection of symmetry as a constituent of geometry is very easily appreciated, and is highly desirable as a contrast to man's apparent imperfections. Symmetry in the Islamic garden very often takes a bilateral or mirror-image form, such as a central channel around which the elements of the garden are disposed. A square or rectangular, rather than a non-rectangular or freely-disposed, layout is among the chief characteristics of the Islamic garden and courtyard. A focal point, such as a fountain set in a shallow bowl in the centre of a patio, or a mausoleum at the centre of a large garden with side pavilions terminating secondary vistas, also expresses an order and logic and has universal appeal. The symmetrical plan of courtyard and garden can give a great sense of satisfaction and accomplishment. Typically, of a stream that flowed through a garden he acquired near Kabul, Babur, the first Mughal Emperor, recounted that 'formerly its course was zig-zag and irregular; I had it made straight and orderly; so the place became very beautiful'.

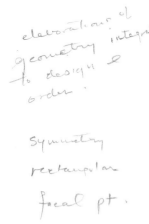

31 Sky, building and foliage reflected in the water of an ablution pool in the garden of the Mader-i Shah Medersa, Isfahan. Such effects had a more than merely picturesque appeal. Deep water, dark, mysterious and still, was a powerful image of eternity.

41

32 The highly decorated ceiling in the
porch of the Chehel Sutun at Isfahan, a
royal pavilion dating in its present form
from the early 18th century. Although wood
was a luxury in Iran, this lavish pleasure-
house contains fluted cedar columns as well
as wood beams, coffers, painted louvres and
inlay work of rosettes, suns and stars.

33 A fountain basin of carved marble set
on a raised platform in the centre of a grass
yard at the fort in Lahore. The stone and
marble surround to the basin has a
rectilinear pattern of star formations in sharp
contrast to the flowing tendril of the basin
itself.

42

34 Polychrome tile paving on a platform overlooking a courtyard in the Bardo Palace at Algiers. Although of a relatively late date, the interwoven border forming the star pattern is characteristic of an ordering element recurring throughout the centuries.

35 Stone paving in a courtyard at the Alcazar in Seville. Pattern is the unifying element in all Islamic art. Geometry, line, texture and colour all contribute to a single effect.

Below right
37 One of the deep pools of the hilltop city of Fatehpur Sikri. It was once widely assumed that a shortage of water led to the eventual abandonment of the city, but this now seems not to be the case; there is an elaborate water supply system, most of which is well preserved.

36 An octagonal pool at a four-way intersection of runnels in the garden of the Tomb of Humayun at Delhi. This square garden is divided by broad causeways, and further subdivided by paths into smaller squares. The whole orderly geometry and symmetry of the garden is seen in microcosm in this illustration.

Facing page

38 Arcade bounding the courtyard of the Ibn Youssef Medersa in Marrakesh. The regular rhythm of the columns and arches encloses a rich series of structured geometrical and flowing patterns in faience, carved stucco and wood.

39 A garden in the *zenana* quarter of the Amber Palace near Jaipur, exhibiting both Mughal and Rajput influence. The basin in the centre was once water-filled, with bridges leading to the stone platform. The stone parterre is based upon the star, which symbolized both life and intellect.

40 Sunlit courtyard of the Bahia Palace in Marrakesh. The central placing of fountain basin and symmetrical arcade, mosaic-tiled paving in geometrical patterns and doors of inlaid wood show how design traditions established centuries earlier continued almost until our own times.

41 Another view of the Bahia Palace, Marrakesh. Beyond these enclosed courtyards stretches an extensive garden.

In addition to the search for the universal, there was also an awareness of the particular character of a site. The choice of sites, from the hillsides of Andalusia or Kashmir to the river banks of Agra, and even the paradise gardens deliberately created as contrast within the dry plains of Iran, often seem to reflect an intuitive romanticism.

Buildings, walls, arcades, axial pathways, steps, straight canals and parterres are in complete contrast to the background of bushes, trees and free foliage; they set the context for the organic growth of the planting they define. Flowers are planted informally, and with shrubs and trees often overhang the eges of paths and channels. The theme of a strictly controlled man-made geometry that bounds an organic form is also to be seen in other manifestations of Islamic art. One example is the design of arabesques in the dome of the Masjid-i Shah at Isfahan, another the inlay of semi-precious stone representing plants set in the walls of the Taj Mahal at Agra.

Indeed, within the plants themselves there is also an inherent geometry: in the flower heads, in the individual petals and in the veins of leaves. Apart from very slight modification due to wind, heat, cold and factors of a similar nature that affected the plant during its growth, all parts are balanced. This was not lost on the Muslim. Yet remarkably, although there is similarity in design, there is no uniformity. The Islamic garden still reflects a spirit based on the individual organic growth of its various natural components.

Are there other ways by which order and unity are achieved? Climate determines the degree of shade that is sought and what will grow, thus subtly unifying the range of plants within a particular garden. Terrain can impose a series of terraces and waterfalls, or determine that an axis culminate in a river view. Order induced by repetition will be seen, for example, in a double line of cypress trees that define an axis, or in a unified pattern of paving slabs extending across a courtyard, while the defined and enclosed space of a courtyard itself clearly imposes its own order.

Order:
other determinants

42 A view of the Patio de los Naranjos, Seville, originally the courtyard of the Mosque. The strict formation of the orange trees enables them to be watered easily by a system of channels. The photograph is taken from the Giralda, the old minaret, which substantially survives.

43   A single central channel at Verinag in Kashmir, nearly 300 metres long, carries water from the octagonal pool to a waterfall at the garden's boundary in the far distance. Its strong lines are emphasized by the flanking paths. The upper end of this channel may be seen in plate 193.

44   A view of the long channel that leads through the centre of the Patio de la Acequia of the Generalife at Granada. The planting on all sides is grouped informally, but its extent is rigorously defined by straight paths.

45   Detail of the parterres surrounding the central reservoir at Shalamar Bagh, Lahore. Besides defining areas of vegetation, the parterres as a whole also act as borders to the garden's central reservoir. The shape of the parterres may be compared with those seen bordering the canal in plate 68.

46 On a spur of the mountains overlooking Dal Lake in Kashmir is Pari Mahal, or 'The Fairies' Palace'. The garden is composed of a series of terraces. Structurally it is in poor condition, but the location and the views it affords remain entrancing.

The task of co-ordinating a multiplicity of elements into an ordered system or unified vision is invariably that of the artist. To pursue this objective in the design of a garden, each component should retain its individual identity, yet combine into a coherent whole. It was the task of the designer of the Islamic garden both to provide those elements that gave pleasure and comfort while reflecting the Islamic paradise image, and to combine all into a comprehensive and fundamental order in keeping with Islamic precepts. The result was a rich and refined vocabulary that extended across the Islamic world.

Space

Space may be conceived as all-pervading. To the orthodox Muslim it flows both out to the Heavens to encompass the Divine Spirit, and in to the soul. However, the interpretation of space in the Islamic world is not exclusively mystical, nor even symbolic. To be aware of it in its various dimensions remains a biological process, while its conscious definition is the function of the artist and architect, who shape space for its effect on the observer.

The spaces achieved within such buildings as La Mezquita at Cordova, the Mosque of Suleiman at Istanbul or the Masjid-i Jami at Isfahan, form a significant part of the Muslim heritage; but the Islamic architect did not restrict himself solely to the design of space within a building. A similar process of creation and definition took place with external space open to the sky. Once it was defined by walls or buildings, trees or any three-dimensional object, this external space was no longer abstract, but became a 'place', and possessed its own particular character.

Such a sense of place is a strong attribute of the Islamic garden, where there is a close relationship to the site. Magnificent settings were provided for the Alhambra and Generalife overlooking Granada, for Shah Goli on its hillside near Tabriz, for Pari Mahal above Dal Lake and for Akbar's Tomb garden set in the midst of the plains at Sikandra. The list could be easily extended.

The concept of place implies a space defined by a boundary. In the Islamic garden and courtyard such a space is invariably created by walls. Even when the walls contain accommodation, the rooms derive their light, air and view from the space enclosed, which still retains its primary significance. The effect of this enclosed space is heightened by the location of the entry into the garden. Entry is normally on the central axis, and at the lowest level when the garden is terraced. Such location creates instant maximum effect and clearly determines the view of the space that the observer is expected to take. The occasional departures from square or rectangular layouts are due to exigencies of adjacent ownerships, as at the Alcazar at Seville, or, exceptionally, to terrain, as at Velez Benaudalla.

Scale in the Islamic garden varies. It can provide a sense of immediacy and containment, such as at Chashma Shahi, Kashmir, or one of charming intimacy, such as at San Giovanni degli Eremiti, Palermo. It can contain long internal vistas, as at the Bagh-i Eram, Shiraz, or lead the eye to seemingly limitless distance, as of Dal Lake from Nishat Bagh in Kashmir.

The part played by water in the creation of place can assume many forms. At the Tomb of Moulay Ismail at Meknès, the sole focus of composition in each courtyard is a fountain. At Shalamar Bagh, Lahore, the scale of the tank, organized and disciplined, but not large, acts as focus for the whole garden. Water in a tank is usually still; full to the brim, it clearly reflects the sky or a surrounding arcade, and so creates an ambivalent quality between reality and image, while also extending the dimensions of a place.

XIII

XIV

47 Groups of columned kiosks (*chhatri*) with cupola roofs rise magically above the red sandstone wall enclosing the fort at Agra. Here the grace of the carved white marble contrasts most effectively with the large stone blocks at its base, creating a sense of enclosure and mystery.

48 A garden set like a living raft upon the waters of a lake, seen from a window in the Amber Palace, near Jaipur.

49 The sunlit courtyard and basin of the
Bou Inaniye Medersa, Fez, seen through an
entry arch containing a carved cedarwood
doorway.

50 At the highest level of Nishat Bagh,
Kashmir, is the *zenana* terrace, its edge
bounded by a wall. This is the largest of the
gardens on Dal Lake; behind it rise the
mountain ranges of the north.

51 Outside the garden surrounding the ⟩
Tomb of Itimad-ud-Daula, at Agra, is an
orchard dating from the days of the
Timurids, which extends from its main gate
to the road. Walled orchards were often
attached to significant gardens, the sale of
their produce covering the gardens' upkeep
after the owners' deaths. Beyond the outer
wall, pedestrians, rickshaws, bullock carts,
bicycles and trucks jostle each other.

52 A small tank in an enclosure off the garden on the site of San Giovanni degli Eremiti in Palermo. Though built under the Normans, Moorish influence was strong, and the intimate scale of the garden remains evocative of Islam to this day.

53 Carved marble fountain and basin within a courtyard of the Bardo Palace, Algiers. By the time this residence was built at the turn of the 18th century, the rigid symmetry and ordered placing of the various architectural elements had been relaxed, but water still remained the focus of this sunlit, enclosed place.

Frequently, water is employed as an element of continuity throughout the length of a garden, or it leads the eye to a mausoleum or other structure. A long, straight channel of water in the Islamic context possibly symbolizes infinity. In design terms, it gives a sense of direction, as with the grand sheet of water before the Chehel Sutun, Isfahan, or when it points from four sides to the Tombs of Humayun or Itimad-ud-Daula. Paths and stepping stones by their function also suggest direction.

Linkage between one garden space and another is often achieved through a series of changes in level. Frequently a channel of water forms a string on which tanks, fountains and platforms are strung like beads. Water also forms a continuous link between indoors and out, as at the Alhambra, or between one room and another, as in the Emperor's apartments at the Red Fort, Delhi.

The spaces, terraces and enclosures of the Islamic gardens and courtyards form a link in scale between the precisely defined rooms of dwellings, tombs and palaces, and the irregular enclosures of the orchards and fields, plains and forests, mountains and valleys of the wider landscape that surround them. An established pattern of connection, such as the street, which leads via a transitional element, perhaps an entrance lobby, to a climax – the actual garden or courtyard – provides a continuity of spatial experience found in almost every case. The customary route for the garden's visitor leads through changes of level, and past a line of trees, a colonnaded pavilion, or an inclined plane of tumbling water, all of which provide a further range of spatial experience.

59

54   Causeways containing channels bisect the Hayat Baksh Bagh in the Red Fort at Delhi. The square garden is divided into four, and each quadrant is similarly divided again. The subtle play of levels, never varying by more than a few centimetres, and of textures – grass, marble, water – makes it an abstract composition of endless interest.

55   Water flows through the Diwan-i-Am, past stepping stones and under a seating platform before it falls over a cascade and into a pool at the foot of the Shalamar Bagh, Kashmir. No European garden brings man and water into such totally unified communion. The reverse view is seen in plate 106.

Form

56   A miniature bridge leads directly to a small central pavilion in the garden at Achabal, Kashmir. On each side are pools with fountains, the abundance of the water seemingly only restricted by the cut stone.

57   A series of doorways links the various rooms and courtyards of the Khas Mahal, alternating light and darkness, coolness and warmth. This view is similar to the view through the Emperor's private apartments at the Red Fort in Delhi.

Within the garden, views are guided not only from the point of entry but in specific directions following axes defined by water channels. These are paralleled by paths, parterres and trees, and occasionally elaborated by intermediate paths or water chutes. When the observer is seated in a central pavilion or on a platform over a channel, his view is strictly axial. Even progress through the garden follows what amounts to a prescribed route. To walk through the remainder of the garden is less common, and any views off-axis are largely obtained when seated on the grass, under trees. Although the views of a courtyard from its entry point, its surrounding rooms or its arcade are frequently off-axis, consistently these views are static too, since the observer of a courtyard or patio is nearly always seated. In sum, the clear definition of space and its orderly perception are among the most noticeable characteristics of the Islamic garden and courtyard.

The form of a garden is influenced by tradition and culture. Long before Islam four elements were considered sacred: water, fire, air and earth. The book of Genesis recounts that 'a river went out of Eden to water the garden; and from thence it was parted, and became four heads'. In Persian ceramics dating back approximately six thousand years, the world is depicted as divided into four sections by two axes that form a cross. At the focal point is a pool, or Spring of Life. This image may be related to the mandala of Buddhist iconography, and reflects a view of the universe and symbol of life that, possibly commencing in Iran, spread throughout the *Dar-al-Islam*. The symbol of four rivers, which branch out from a common source or centre in the direction of the four cardinal points, stands for fertility and timelessness. This image was even embodied in

58   A magnificent portal or gateway often marked the entry to an Islamic garden, or terminated an internal axial vista. This highly ornamental gateway, set in an otherwise unadorned wall, leads to the Tomb of Moulay Ismail in Meknès.

Facing page
59   A crenellated wall defines the Mamounia Gardens at Marrakesh, and protects its orange groves, olive trees and kitchen gardens from the surrounding city.

60   From one of the marble terraces near the Baghdad Kiosk in the north-west corner of Topkapi Saray, Istanbul, one looks down upon a simply designed rectangular pool shaded by willow trees.

early game preserves or hunting grounds (which were also divided into four parts with a mansion at the intersection), as well as in the courtyard, with its fountain or pool at the centre, and also quite clearly in the quadripartite garden (*char bagh*); only in later gardens did the symbol tend to disappear. Similarly, the flow of a river symbolizes not only fertility but the passage of time, while bathing in a sacred river was equivalent to losing the self and achieving salvation in the ocean of existence.

Although the dimensions of the Garden of Paradise were those of heaven and earth, its terrestrial Islamic counterpart was wall-enclosed (the Quran mentions gates), since, in addition to defining a particular place, a walled garden or an enclosed courtyard was a valued refinement in a dry land. Protection was afforded from the encroaching sand, and from the noise and bustle of the city. High walls, trees and shrubs afforded privacy and a place for spiritual contemplation. Outside was the barren landscape, the heat and the glare; inside was shade and vegetation, symbolizing life. This was where one could hear the rustling of leaves, the murmur and splash of water, and the occasional intonation of prayer.

The shape of a particular garden in the *Dar-al-Islam* will be determined by climate, terrain and amount of land available, as well as by the personal desires of the owner working within the customary geometry; yet it will share a number of themes with the very early garden concepts. Entry is often through a magnificent portal or gateway. The plan is rectangular, and based on an idealized pattern of irrigation in which water is both physically and symbolically the source of life. The main axis is formed by a water course, often higher than the surrounding ground, flanked by paths, bordered with trees and sometimes crossed by one or more secondary axes at right angles. These secondary axes either also carry water or are simply walks. Flowers and trees are often located in the quadrants. As we have seen, the four water channels not only symbolize the four rivers of life, but to a Muslim their intersection also represents the meeting of man and God. Symbolism combines easily with practicality to provide irrigation and refreshing vegetation. A pavilion or other form of building is usually located at the centre of the garden, where the coolness of the water can be enjoyed. Sometimes a building terminates a side vista. In either case, the structure is located to provide an attractive view and a setting for conversation.

There are various types of Islamic garden. Palaces may contain a large walled garden, such as a *char bagh*, which surrounds a pavilion or, occasionally, the palace itself. A palace may also contain an inner court garden. There are larger areas used for sports; and in addition there may be vineyards, orchards and kitchen gardens. There are pleasure gardens that simply contain a pavilion, while in India there are gardens that the owner could enjoy not only during his lifetime, but later when they contained his mausoleum, since it was believed that, after his death, he had already symbolically entered Paradise.

Many of the attributes of the Islamic garden are shared by the courtyard. The bustle of the streets and the cries of the bazaar are excluded, in this case, not solely by a wall but also by the surrounding building. Thus isolated, its shape defined by the dwelling, the courtyard becomes a hidden treasure, a restful place, devoid of tension and encouraging contemplation. The conception of this space was static, and reflected equilibrium and repose; each area, even each arcade, was sufficient within itself. Despite the frequent decorative richness of the architecture, the simple austerity of the basic building form is not overwhelmed; and in the centre of the courtyard, flooded

Facing page

61 The courtyard of the large Masjid-i Jami in Isfahan. An enclosing two-storey arcade forms the sides of a square with a large *iwan* (entry portal) in the centre of each of the four sides; in the middle of the courtyard is the basin for ablutions. This is one of the earliest examples of a plan that was to become characteristic of Iranian mosque courtyards.

62 Elaborate, carved marble fountain centre-piece in a pool next to the Revan Kiosk at Topkapi Saray, Istanbul. A view of the jets around the edge of this pool may be seen in plate 234.

63 *Chini-kana* of white marble in the Sawan pavilion within the Red Fort at Delhi. This was originally behind a waterfall and the niches would have been filled with candles or flowers.

64 Water flowing under and around a stone *chabutra* placed in the central canal at Shalamar Bagh, Kashmir. One sat on cushions, the sound of flowing water in one's ears, surrounded by moist, cool air amid the heat of summer.

with light, there was the inevitable splashing fountain or straight-sided pool, where ablutions were performed before prayer began.

Sloping terrain normally entailed a series of terraces. In the large royal gardens, the lowest terrace is used solely for public receptions, the middle is private and reserved for men and the upper (*zenana*) terrace is for women. A pavilion or, more simply, a stone seat mark a change of level. Where water is involved, there is a cascade (often over carved niches bearing flowers or lamps), or alternatively a carved chute that leads into a channel or terminates in a basin. The water pressure generated is used for fountains. Where there is no natural slope, an artificial gradient may be created to ensure a flow of water. And as a major element of the Islamic garden, water is always given a well-defined shape.

65 Path defining the junction between a pool and canal at Shalamar Bagh, Lahore. When the water level is low, it flows from one area to the next along the minor channels seen on the left. When the level rises, it flows through a series of apertures underneath the path.

66 A round fluted fountain basin of white marble set in the floor of the pavilion at the highest end of Shalamar Bagh, Lahore. It is surrounded by a square border of coloured stone and marble inlay, set slightly below floor level.

67 A hexagonal pool contains a finely carved, tiered fountain of marble in the north-west corner of the original tulip garden at the foot of the Baghdad Kiosk at Topkapi Saray, Istanbul. This form of tiered fountain, seen earlier in plate 20, came late to Islamic gardens, and is more characteristic of Turkey than elsewhere.

68　The mid-19th-century Zafar Mahal, framed by columns of the Sawan pavilion in the Red Fort at Delhi. Originally in the centre of the Hayat Baksh Bagh, the Zafar Mahal was set in a red sandstone tank intended for bathing. Like many other Islamic gardens, the absence of water deprives it of much of its living beauty.

Plants and water are both inherently more complex than the static man-made forms around them; plants grow and water moves, each according to its own natural laws. The solidity and stability of the land with its man-made structures, and the fluidity of the water, even when geometrically confined, form the greatest of contrasts. During the dry season, when some gardens are devoid of water, man-made geometry is dominant, although the presence of water is still suggested by the shapes of the canal edges, tanks, chutes and fountain-heads; once the water flows, the atmosphere becomes exuberant and the garden comes to life again.

Since paths are usually at a level higher than the surrounding garden, the geometrical character of the layout is emphasized, the surrounding vegetation is prevented from obscuring the architecture and one has the illusion of walking at the level of a floral carpet. Paths are always straight, and never at random; their vistas are controlled and lead to a pavilion, kiosk, gateway or *iwan*. Path surfaces are paved with brick, stone or pebbles or occasionally mosaic. Invariably the geometry of the layout and the hard edges of the building materials are softened by the organic quality of the planting.

Avenues are lined with trees, usually the evergreen cypress which represents immortality. Trees that blossom in the spring represent a renewal of life. Trees, myrtle bushes and other overhanging vegetation give shade, and help prevent excessive loss of moisture through evaporation. Throughout the garden, fruit trees predominate and, together with vines, help to shade the plants.

69 Hexagonal stone paving in the garden of the Nematollah Valli Shrine at Mahan, near Kerman: a simple geometrical pattern carried out in an unsophisticated way.

Flowers do not play a major role, although roses and jasmine are common. When not scattered across the grass or planted formally in parterres, they are often grouped in earthenware pots or vases. Flowers are fully represented in Persian miniatures, Persian and Mughal carpets, Turkish pottery, Mughal manuscripts and in the marble inlay of Mughal buildings. As for the rose, it has been described for centuries by Iranian poets as the perfect manifestation of the glory of God.

Further contributions to the garden come from coloured tiles, which are placed on walls, balustrades and other vertical surfaces. There is also the song of birds. The nightingale is most sought after, and in Iran there were once nightingale gardens where cages hung in the trees. But tradition strongly discouraged statuary.

The form of the Islamic garden, its layout and planting, and the treatment and detailing of its water, faithfully reflect the ever-present symbolism and overriding geometry of Islamic art. The geometric ordered layout in particular provides a profound sense of association with a spirit, or with ideas, felt to be greater than man himself.

Texture

To the contemplative Muslim, the surface of an object can have a transcendent quality owing both to the richness of the material and to its pattern. One may easily imagine how some materials such as a richly veined marble can attain this quality; and one may also appreciate how it can be achieved through a geometrical pattern that interconnects shapes and colours. Texture can also help a substance lose its appearance of weight, and so achieve a desirable spiritual quality.

Texture refers to surface characteristics. It implies many small units brought together as one. Some materials, such as stone and wood, possess their own inherent texture, even when finished in a variety of ways. Texture emerges from the surface of a shape. Since any surface may be felt, some form of texture is always present.

Texture may also be seen, its nature changing with distance. For example, from afar, a mass of trees and a body of water almost merge into one, as at one of the lakeside gardens in Kashmir; somewhat closer, pavilions and foliage become distinguishable; while closer still, even individual flower petals, the water surface, the variation of leaves and the texture of earth are appreciated.

Catching the eye and modelling light, texture creates an infinite number of highlights and shadows. The Muslim artist and architect fully realized that the innate qualities of a shape could be enhanced or obscured by texture. Smoothness is comfortable, but slipperiness is troublesome. A degree of roughness can also be attractive, but if too strong can be aggressive, and detract from the shape beneath. In the Islamic garden and courtyard, although there is usually a great deal of intricacy, there is little rough texture. Its particular quality and scale would be out of place, and would also detract from the clearly defined geometry of the whole. On the other hand, there are many smooth and matte surfaces, such as tiled paving and stuccoed wall, and these provide the added delight of reflecting gradations of light and shade.

The nature of texture in the Islamic garden and courtyard varies. An applied texture simply accepts the nature of a particular material, and proceeds to maintain or heighten it. A clear example of this is the marble of a Mughal tomb, polished to reveal its inherent grain. A development is an applied texture that

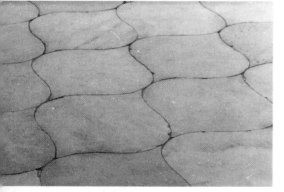

70 White marble paving at the Red Fort in Delhi: the same instinct for pattern, but here executed in the most subtle of shapes, neatly meshed in a net of curving lines. Yet it remains a surface on which to walk.

modifies the material, but does not transform it unduly. The intricate carving of a Moroccan wood screen illustrates such an approach. By contrast, small pieces of a material are frequently organized into a pattern, and with their joints form an entirely new surface texture. The pebble paths of Andalusia, the mosaic tile of North Africa, and the sandstone and marble inlay of Mughal India illustrate this aspect. In such cases, while the materials remain identifiable, the character of the new surface created is more dominant than that intrinsically possessed by the material itself.

The texture of paths and terraces in the Islamic garden vary from smooth marble to worn sandstone and brick. Besides these there is the texture of the joints and their pattern in relation to the geometry of the panels and inlaid walls. Sometimes there are narrow strips of grass between the paving stones, or, alternatively, narrow stones are set in extensive lawns. Wide stone platforms sometimes contain parterres. In these situations, texture not only modulates the quality of solids, but influences the nature of the place. Smooth surfaces are generally to be found where people walk or sit; for example, grassed areas are flat, stone paths are smooth and courtyards are tiled.

It is not known what emphasis was placed on the texture of flowers in the Islamic garden, although lists of the flowers planted were often given. It may be assumed that roses and jasmine were planted, primarily for scent, but other flowers and plants have no doubt been changed over the years by successive generations of gardeners. Whatever the variety, the spring blossoms and green leaves that appeared after the barrenness of winter must always have provided a lively interest and attractive textural foil to the wood, stone and marble of garden buildings. The cypresses of Andalusia, the palms of Morocco and the chenars and willows of Kashmiri gardens have their own distinctive textures.

71 A highly elaborate example of carved stucco relief surrounds a doorway in the Alhambra, Granada. Contrasting patterns are juxtaposed in clearly defined panels, those above the door imitating the shapes of voussoirs. The crisp carving reads clearly in the strong sunlight.

72 Water splashes over a marble basin into a star-shaped shallow pool in the courtyard of the Dar Batha Palace in Fez, the mosaic tile surround glistening with the spray.

73 The rectangular slabs are carved tombstones set in the ground within a radiating pattern of smaller round and cut stones. This treatment of the floor surface is to be found within the courtyard of the Shiite Shrine of Shah Zadeh Huseyn at Qasvin.

74 The type of path seen here at Nishat Bagh in Kashmir is also to be found in other gardens in the region. By allowing grass to grow between the worn stone flags, they become integrated with the smooth lawns and flower beds on either side.

75 An interlocking pattern in brick in the garden of the Tomb of Jahangir, Lahore. The technique of brick paving was traditional to the city, and may also be seen in plate 200. This particular example is from a raised causeway in the garden of the mausoleum.

Facing page
76 A rectangular pool in the courtyard of the Sahrij Medersa in Fez reflects the texture of carved wood screens and polychrome faience on its motionless surface.

77 A variety of vegetation springs from the thick mud a little below the surface of Dal Lake, Kashmir. Here, reeds and water lilies anchor cloud reflections in the still water. A floating island, used for market gardening, lies beyond.

So do the fruit trees – orange and lemon, plum and apple, pomegranate and almond.

Together with the textures of hard building materials and planting, the texture of water contributes in significant measure. In a tank it can be quite still; but the mirror-like surface of a quiet pool can soon be disturbed by the patter of raindrops in Andalusia, a light breeze in the courtyard of a Moroccan *medersa*, ripples from a diving kingfisher in Kashmir, or the spray and swirl from a fountain. By contrast, a swift-flowing channel can become a bright curved sheet as it pours over a waterfall, or become further broken and aerated by a carved *chadar*. Flowing down a carved inclined plane, the water becomes not merely linked to the architecture, but a part of it. The carving is often elaborate, and the textured stone or marble *chadar* forms ridges, chevrons, scallops or dishes. This texture, especially in Mughal India, results in one of the most distinctive elements of the Islamic garden.

78 Scalloped carving of a *chadar* (water-chute) in Nishat Bagh, Kashmir. Chutes were carved to break up into foam the sheet of water that flowed over them. Each of the large number of *chadars* in this garden is carved to a different pattern.

79 A *chadar* in full spate at Nishat Bagh, Kashmir. The spray helps moisten and cool the air, while the constant tumbling and splash provide a pleasing background to the song of the birds and sound of human voices.

80 The carving of a *chadar* could be of amazing delicacy. This detail is of the white marble chute in the Shah Bagh pavilion in the Red Fort at Delhi. The texture, designed to break the flow of the water, is of a more rounded nature than the usual simple patterns. The context of this chute may be seen in plate 175.

Facing page
81 Floral design in a fountain basin in the Emperor's apartments of the Red Fort at Delhi. The inner and outer borders once contained multicoloured stones. Each of the other three borders has as its basis a fan-shaped shell. The complete basin may be seen in plate 93.

82 Sunken basin in the Musamman Bagh of the fort at Agra. The ripples of its semi-precious stone inlay are like those left by the retreating tide, while in the centre is a swirl simulating that of water.

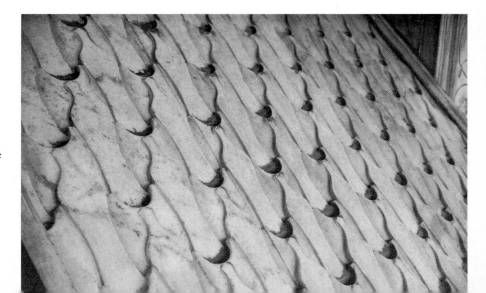

Pattern

Muslims regard the beauty of the world as ephemeral. The realistic portrayal of people and animals was not of interest, and, because of the risk of idolatry, could be even blasphemous. Creative imagination consequently turned to abstract motifs, which then became highly developed. Primary themes were geometrical patterns reflecting the unity of the universe through control of interlocking forms; symbolized plant and natural forms signifying fertility and abundance; and calligraphic compositions, expressing the words and glory of Allah. Individual detail was secondary to overall pattern and repetition, a principle strengthened by tradition and the spiritual values of the Quran.

The artistic heritage of the Arabs themselves was slight, and the strength of Islamic art derives principally from the traditions of the peoples drawn into the Islamic fold. These traditions were adapted to express the desired abstract patterns, rhythms and repetitions, and developed to transform all suitable surfaces. Gradually, the various contributing artistic strands evolved and merged into a unified vocabulary that clearly expressed many of the tenets of Islamic culture.

Facing page far left
83 Lines of white marble define an interwoven geometric pattern in the sandstone paving of the Tomb of Humayun at Delhi. Comparable patterns are found on the walls, windows, grilles and balustrading of the mausoleum, their intricate flow typical of Islamic design.

84 Interlocking sandstone and marble slabs of the platform on which the Taj Mahal is placed; the pattern is repeated in the terrace at its foot. The two types of stone contrast strongly in texture and colour, yet the overall effect is sufficiently simple not to detract from the quality of the mausoleum above. The context of this paving may be seen in plate 169.

85 Part of the floor of the upper chamber of the Tomb of Itimad-ud-Daula at Agra. Black marble and yellow porphyry are set in white marble in bold leaf-scroll pattern, possibly influenced by the Iranian background of Nur Jahan who commissioned the design.

Facing page left
86 A wall in the Alhambra, Granada. The lower part is lined with mosaic tile in white, red, yellow, blue and green. The sequence of tile at the base, stucco in the centre and wood at the top is characteristic of much Islamic architecture. In this example, interweaving geometric, plant and calligraphic patterns are all evident.

87 The practical purpose of these channels, set into the Patio de los Naranjos, Seville, is to water the orange trees planted there. However, the geometrically abstract pattern that they form, together with the brick paving laid in diagonal formation, creates a level of interest of its own.

88 A variety of geometric patterns in stone and marble defines the surface of the courtyard of the Sultan Hassan Mosque in Cairo, like a series of luxurious carpets. The rich but subdued colour of this surface contrasts effectively with the sombre stone and stucco of the surrounding structure.

When Islamic pattern is developed on a single plane, it is very clear, and its quality, simplicity and limited use of materials and techniques reflect a unified concept of the whole, and an understanding that man's existence is a part of the greater design of the universe. When pattern is developed at a multiplicity of levels, the nature of the material seems transformed, and the designs encourage contemplation. Interrelated layers of Islamic pattern reflect interrelated and hierarchical levels of understanding, in the manner that experience and memory, for example, enrich the basic personality. Complex patterns hold the interest longer than simple ones. Not only do they demonstrate a greater ingenuity, but they also incidentally testify to an energy and labour that throughout the *Dar-al-Islam* was available to spare on such a field as artistic ornament, and through this to the enrichment of life itself.

89 A column in the arcade surrounding the courtyard of the Bou Inaniye Medersa at Meknès. On each side are two intricately carved wooden screens. The column itself is faced with coloured faience in a simple geometric pattern, surmounted by the customary calligraphic inscription. A little above this, carved in stucco, is a further inscription with interwoven floral decoration.

90 A path of hexagonal paving stones set into the earth leads between rhododendron bushes in the fourth court at Topkapi Saray, Istanbul.

91 Varied colours of marble, inlaid along the base of a channel at the Red Fort in Delhi. The chevron pattern – its double direction emphasized here by little flowers, perhaps to symbolize the flow of water – is often found in Islamic design.

Arab ability in mathematics encouraged the exploration and development of abstract pattern, but although such pattern was to develop in a highly structured manner, it remained fluid and creative throughout. Line and circle were imaginatively elaborated. Checkerboard and chevrons, and interlocking bands in star and polygonal configurations are employed, as well as knots, medallions and rosettes, and many other motifs. The same designs run not only across the stone, marble and tiles of buildings, but through carpets, metalware and books. They transform the surface and make it ethereal.

The pattern most associated with Islamic art is perhaps the vine tendril, with its innumerable waves, spirals and loops. Originating as a fairly realistic representation of vine leaves and grapes, reflecting fecundity, it soon became stylized, and its eventual total abstraction was specifically an Arab contribution. Extremely adaptable, it became a pattern with a great number of variants, although it was always portrayed as an organic part of the plant form. Waves, leafy scrolls and branches interlace in a continuous flowing rhythm; infinitely flexible, the pattern is applied to areas of all manner of shapes, as overall motif, as frieze or border, or simply as background to calligraphy. Other patterns derived from organic forms are the acanthus, palmette and highly stylized rosette. Later patterns of plant form, although retaining an abstract form of grouping, reverted to a more naturalistic rendering, and pomegranates, pine cones and individual flower forms became clearly recognizable.

One particular element that was uniquely adapted to decorative surface enrichment was Arabic calligraphy. Written in a wide variety of forms from angular Kufic to round and flowing Naskhi, it is used not only in books but on buildings and even extended to otherwise humble domestic articles. Normally, texts from the Quran were chosen to adorn Islamic buildings, although the occasional word of praise for ruler or benefactor is also found, accompanied by a modest reference to the owner or his architect. The richly inventive and often playful calligraphic flourishes, integrating completely with the surrounding geometric and flowing abstract ornament, also help to transform all appropriate surfaces; yet the script throughout remains quite legible.

Islamic ornament is used to define and emphasize functional and component elements to which it relates in scale and character. Pattern is appropriate to its location. For example, the enrichment and elaboration of a doorway to a garden emphasizes the link between inside and out, and prepares the observer for the experience of passing through; while a star or regular polygon centred in the mosaic around a courtyard fountain suggests a place to linger. Throughout the courtyard as a whole, the use of pattern emphasizes the predominant horizontal dimension of this space. Garden pavilions and tombs, as with other Islamic buildings, contain a full range of surface enrichment. Curling floral decoration is easily adapted to any shaped surface, and carved on many a marble basin; while a chevron pattern, symbolizing flowing water, can appropriately form the floor of a channel. The lozenge pattern round garden water tanks very possibly derives from log ends of earlier construction.

At first sight, Islamic pattern may seem to be entirely a subject of independent whim. Yet the designer operated wholly within the tradition of his art, within the limitations of his materials, the demands of the market and the overall restraints of Islamic culture. Far from regarding the use of pattern as excessive, a contemplative Muslim will delight in its intricacy, and read it as if it were a poem, full of inherent interest and endless innovation.

92 Detail of the basin in the Musamman Bagh at the fort at Agra, seen earlier in plate 82. Plant forms and the curving tendril flow round the surfaces in flat inlay, low relief or fully realized three-dimensional carving.

93 Fountain basin in the Emperor's apartments of the Red Fort at Delhi. The calyx itself of this full lotus of twenty-four petals forms a basin. Scented water once brimmed over the bud in the centre.

Light Fire, air, water and earth constitute the four elements, but it was fire alone, through its ability to mature and redefine, that was considered to bring all things into harmony. A significant aspect of fire, apart from heat, is light. In the strong sunshine generally experienced throughout the Islamic world, light is of great consequence. The sun, and subsequently pure light, symbolized the Absolute Being, since its illumination is the source of all existence. The sun gives life by its rays and through its light everything is rendered apparent. Pure light is indivisible, and represents the Muslim's sense of universal order.

Three aspects of light may be relevant here. The first, the cognitive, aspect is related to perception, and reveals and defines the environment in terms of shape, brightness and colour. In a sense, when an object such as a garden or courtyard is designed, light is affected and any adjustment modulates this light. A garden or courtyard may in this way be regarded as a visible form built of various light qualities. The second aspect is aesthetic, and is related to sensual and emotional awareness, originally stemming from the sun, moon and stars. The third aspect of light is the symbolic, linking both cognitive and aesthetic aspects, and assisting in providing life itself with meaning and unity. This aspect of light is metaphorically associated with life, goodness, truth and order. In sum, light leads to an understanding of the world, while it adds immeasurably to the joy of living.

In any specific place, the light always has a unique quality. This particular nature of the light becomes associated with a specific region, a landscape, its buildings and its gardens. It has always played a significant role in the shape of objects, their texture and colour. Yet while the shape of land, and to some extent water, may be exactly determined and controlled, the variability of daylight has to be accepted by artist and architect.

The architect concerns himself with light as a form of energy to be manipulated for human comfort; but he is also interested in controlling light as a major constituent of the spaces he has created. He does this because it contributes to the appreciation of his building by people, and to the enjoyment they derive from it. Inside a building, mood may be greatly influenced by the quality, intensity and direction of light; in Islamic buildings, it is often filtered through a screen (*jali*).

94 A detail from a window of the Tomb of Itimad-ud-Daula in Agra. Openings in this mausoleum are screened with an intricate marble lattice, which diffuses the light into the interior. The geometric detail of this screen echoes the complexity of the inlay technique employed for the walls, as seen in plate 10.

95   Filtered sunlight streams through screens in the Emperor's apartments at the Red Fort, Delhi. The preceding screen at the Tomb of Itimad-ud-Daula is more elaborately carved, but its context is similar to that illustrated here. Marble and sandstone were both used for such screens.

96   Also at Delhi's Red Fort is this finely carved marble screen, almost unbelievable in its delicacy, that separates the Diwan-i-Khas in the Emperor's apartments from an adjacent sunlit courtyard. A channel flowing beneath the screen links the two, assisting the shade in reducing the temperature. This screen (one of the central floral panels is broken) terminates the vista seen later in plate 172.

97   Light floods into the courtyard of the Bou Inaniye Medersa at Meknès, and sharply defines the surrounding carved stucco and woodwork (see plate 89). By comparison, the shadow cast by the high enclosing walls is all the more dense, and welcome.

98 A patch of sunlight in the garden of the Alcazar at Seville clearly defines a fountain basin and its matching pool, defined in its turn by tiles set within the brick path.

99 At Achabal, Kashmir, patches of bright sunlight filtering through the darkness of the surrounding plane trees catch the descending water of a side channel. Broken by the chute, it flows on swiftly through the garden.

100 A carved sandstone fountain at Shalamar Bagh, Kashmir. Its liberally cast spray catches the sunlight, and seems to sprinkle diamonds on the surrounding water surface.

Outside, however, while trees and walls may afford some protection and shade, and surfaces provide varying degrees of reflection, brightness and humidity cannot be controlled, although they play a major part in the garden or courtyard experience. In fact, through most of the Islamic world, the light will often be hard and glaring. Nonetheless, each material found in courtyard and garden – wood, stone, marble, flowers, leaves, grass, earth and water – has its characteristic method of distributing light, reflecting or absorbing it. In courtyards, arcades cast contrasting shadow; while in gardens, brightness alternates with the deep shadows of trees relieved by dappled light filtering through and sparkling off water; as the leaves and water move, the pattern pulsates. Similarly, the sunlight flashes from vertical cascades and horizontal pools, or is filtered through the falling spray of fountains and chutes. The manner in which light is reflected off water depends on the degree of movement. Flat surfaces, ripples and droplets all have characteristic reflections, luminosity, or degrees of brilliance. To the Islamic architect, water in garden and courtyard poses as great a design challenge under the sunlight as do the domes, portals, tiles and pierced screens of his buildings.

The Muslim often preferred a pool to be non-transparent, since its depth was then left to the imagination and it could symbolize infinity. The dark gloomy basin so prevalent in garden and courtyard is therefore quite deliberate. On the other hand, many gardens in Andalusia and Kashmir are (or at least were) fed by the clear waters of streams, and their surface mirrors the

101 Detail of the *chini-kana* (the carved recess behind a waterfall) in an enclosure designed to link the water level of the central reservoir to that of the lowest terrace at Shalamar Bagh, Lahore. The niches are carved out of white marble.

sky, the willows or chenars, the cream stucco and wood or red sandstone and marble pavilions that border the channels. In turn, the light reflecting off the water gives a luminosity to the adjacent buildings, in much the same manner as light bouncing off the surrounding marble platform illuminates the temples of classical Greece. After a fall of rain, when a stone or mosaic floor is itself covered with a film of water, there is an added sparkle and interest. The ground underfoot becomes a reflection of the sky; space has expanded and the artist's vision been more fully realized.

At night, the moon and stars, or the glow of candlelight, give a completely different presence to the Islamic garden. The air is cool, and the rose pergolas and varicoloured parterres give place to dark trees, pale flowers and perfume. The still water of the pools reflects the flow of candles set on tiny rafts. The carved niches behind the cascades, which by day contain vases of flowers, are now filled with lamps which glow and flicker through the sheets of glistening water. On festive occasions, fireworks can turn the diamonds of the myriad of droplets into rubies, amethysts and emeralds.

The presence of light leads to an appreciation of colour. When a dome of turquoise tiles rises above the buff-yellow of the surrounding roofs and walls, the intensity of both colours is heightened by contrast. Similarly the black and white marble and red sandstone of Mughal buildings gain when seen against the soft reds and yellows of the soil. Sometimes the effect is one of fine variations of a single colour; in a white marble garden pavilion, for instance,

102 A four-sided *chini-kana* surrounds the finely carved pool set in the floor of the Bhadon pavilion in the Hayat Baksh Bagh at the Red Fort, Delhi. Water poured into this pool from every direction, and candles were set in these niches, their flames visible through the film of water passing over them.

103 Tiny panels of mirror set in the ceiling reflect light entering the great porch of the Chehel Sutun at Isfahan. Once they also reflected the sparkling water from the fountains and tank set in the floor below.

the material itself gives a subtle sense of depth. Often, especially in tilework, colours are mixed. Warmer colours, such as red and orange, and particularly white and yellow, seem to advance, and these are employed as highlights. Cooler, more subdued colours, such as green, blue and violet, seem to recede, and are used as background. The Muslim artist also saw that lighter colours seem to expand. Contrasting colours placed next to each other are employed in large areas to avoid being diffused by the eye; conversely, analogous colours were interwoven in small areas, and the resulting sensations are quite vibrant.

Colour is a secondary component of architecture, since shape, space and texture may still be experienced without it. As with texture, however, when light is available, colour is always present to some degree. Natural materials, such as clay or marble, contain their own inherent colours; artificial colours are applied through mosaic, faience tile and marble inlay. Architecturally, colour is also used to articulate form and space, and it can endow a focal point, such as the ceiling of a garden pavilion, with particular emphasis. It may also be used to create a rhythm, or to divide a surface, as when it defines the place for prayer (*musalla*) in the floor of a mosque.

Much of the Islamic world is bleak and barren, but in the spring time it becomes radiant with flowers and blossom. The bright light burns the browns and buffs into the barren desert, but the same light also fully reveals the white marble, red sandstone and turquoise tiles of the buildings, and the intense hues of the orange trees, the dark cypress, the roses and the jasmine of the gardens and courtyards.

Movement

Today's visitor to an Islamic garden is fortunately still able to regard it in the way one may assume it was originally meant to be seen – directly and clearly with its formal and axial characteristics predominant. It is, quite apparently, the type of view that was enjoyed by the garden's original occupants, whether these were members of a family taking part in a picnic, business associates who came for earnest conversation, or a Mughal Emperor attended by his courtesans. In every case their perception of the garden was largely static.

But an observer who moves can derive additional pleasure in a number of ways. Apart from the sense of movement itself, the sense of touch, hearing and smell, are all stimulated by walking through the garden. The sedentary observer is conscious of the harmony derived from the water, the straight paths, the flower beds and the trees, but the visitor on foot can also appreciate the continual unfolding of mass, space, light, surface and detail.

This stimulation takes its place in a sequence of experiences appealing both to the sense and to the moving observer's intellectual understanding of the garden's symbolic form. His path may lead first alongside a channel, then up steps and past a pool, then around a pavilion and towards an *iwan*: a changing series of viewpoints, levels and materials. At the beginning of a sequence a gateway marks a clearly determined sense of arrival; at the end, a pavilion or mausoleum gives a sense of completion.

There are further aspects of movement in the garden besides those depending on the motion of the observer. There are natural and climatic forces such as the rare breeze through the leaves, or falling rain. And there are paths, steps and stepping stones – not only do they guide or restrict movement, but they are themselves signs or symbols of motion.

104 View of Shalamar Bagh, Lahore, from the *zenana* terrace, across the great tank with its central platform and still fountains, and between the flanking pavilions which mark the drop to the lowest part of the garden beyond. Originally, as was customary, entry was at the lowest level, so that cascades faced the visitor, and progression was upwards.

Finally, we return yet again to water. Water is the essential source of movement in the Islamic garden and courtyard. One of its basic characteristics is that (apart from evaporation, wind force or mechanical intervention) its movement is determined by gravity. Further, in order to avoid stagnation, it must move continually, although it may well appear still when its lowest possible level has been reached. Water in motion is tireless and ever-changing, and it brings constant life and interest to the environment. In the Islamic garden, it can be exuberant, turbulent and gushing, with much visual turmoil, yet it can also be captive and contained, soothing, and quietly gleaming in the sunlight. The immediacy of the water within a garden contrasts with the obscurity of its source and eventual destination outside, and recalls the natural cycle of water from spring and stream to sea and back again. Within the garden, man-made tank, cascade and channel reflect the lake, waterfall, brook and stream of the natural environment.

105 Stepping stones across the central canal at Shalamar Bagh, Kashmir. They punctuate the flow of water, and allow the visitor an opportunity to enjoy the waterfall's foam, sound and cool air as he crosses them.

Water moves through the Islamic garden in many ways. It changes level over chutes and waterfalls, and spurts into the air from fountains, sending up plumes or bubbling out in sprays and swirls, the droplets pattering on the channels or pools at their base. Falling in the form of sheets or threads, the surface breaks and becomes aerated, filling the air with sound. When water flows through a pavilion, it even introduces a vicarious sense of movement to the static mass of the building itself.

By contrast there is also the stillness of reflecting lakes and quiet pools, whose mirror-like surfaces, as we have seen, encouraged the Muslim in the direction of self-contemplation and revelation. A reflecting pool symbolizes the centre, mirrors the heavens, and unites them with the earth; a dark pool symbolizes the abyss, which meets heaven at the still water's surface.

Part of the experience of moving water is its sound – from the roar of a large cascade or the splashing of fountains to the meditative low gurgling of a gentle stream. In the peaceful Islamic courtyard it is the murmur and trickle of water that is barely audible as it feeds into a pool. But in the garden, water can be heard rippling down carved chutes, cascading over steps, flowing swiftly through channels of cut stone, tumbling into basins, and leaping from jets.

These sounds of water in the Islamic garden are naturally part of the wider context: the buzz of fat bees busily at work along the flower borders, the rustle of willow or the flutter of chenar leaves in a passing breeze, a soft footfall on a path, the glass tinkle of bracelets, the soft patter of a Cordovan shower, or the thundering crash of an Indian monsoon. It is the distinctive combination of such a multitude of particular sounds that contributes to the Islamic garden experience.

Facing page

106   Cascade flowing into a pool in front of the Diwan-i-Am at Shalamar Bagh, Kashmir. A *chabutra*, or stone platform, is seen over the water between the columns. This view is a reverse of that seen in plate 55.

107   Water spilling over a *chadar* at Nishat Bagh, Kashmir. *Chadar* also means a shawl, an analogy that is almost uncannily apt here, with the white foam broken into a soft, lace-like pattern by the carving beneath, and the white foam 'threads' at the base.

108   Fountains throw their spray onto the flowing water round a pavilion in the centre of Shalamar Bagh, Kashmir. The original jets may well have cast solid plumes into the air, rather than sprays.

109   A breeze ruffles the dome of an underwater Taj Mahal, seen here in the pool that surrounds the raised tank in the centre of the *char bagh*.

110   More inverted architecture: water in the ablution pool in the courtyard of the Bou Inaniye Medersa at Meknès reflects the surrounding arcade, and upper level students' rooms. The finely carved stucco and woodwork and calligraphic inscriptions are clearly visible in the still surface.

111   The great porch of the Chehel Sutun at Isfahan is mirrored in the still water of the long reflecting pool that leads from it down the centre of the garden. The name of 'Forty Columns' was given to the pavilion, because its twenty columns were thus doubled by reflection.

Moorish Spain

Setting THE MOORS WERE NORTH AFRICAN converts to Islam, and arrived in Spain early in the 8th century, occupying all the Iberian peninsula except the very northern sector. Following the extinction of the Umayyad dynasty at Damascus, the survivor Abd-ar-Rahman I fled to Andalusia and was crowned independent Emir at Cordova in the mid-8th century. According to Al-Makkari, a historian of the period, one of his first acts was the creation of a garden, which he based on what he had seen at Damascus. Abd-ar-Rahman is reported to have brought plants from India, Turkestan and Syria, and to have introduced into Spain the pomegranate and jasmine, as well as the yellow rose from Iran.

The Iberian peninsula had been the site of Roman villas, and at the time of the Moorish conquest remains of Roman gardens and systems of irrigation were still present. However, the Moors introduced a culture much further advanced in science, art and industry than that generally prevailing in Europe. Cordova became the religious centre of Spain and North Africa, and grew into a large city containing many monuments. Several universities and libraries were founded, and mathematics and medicine made great strides. Bronze, gold, silver and ivory work were exquisitely wrought, and textiles and pottery exported. Design was imaginative, rich and colourful. Yet despite the strong cultural legacy of the Moors, the background of those involved was quite heterogeneous. The Moors themselves were of Arab and Berber stock; there were many Jews, who contributed to mathematics and medicine; there were some Persians; Goths from Italy assisted in the army; and Byzantine Greeks contributed to garden architecture.

By the 10th century, there were reportedly many thousands of gardens in the countryside around Cordova. Laws were passed governing the use of water; baths, aqueducts and systematic irrigation projects were introduced; and luxurious vineyards and orchards were planted throughout Andalusia. Gardens were somewhat smaller than those created in North Africa, but pavilions, arcades and terraces were lined with trees and flowers, and watered from rivers and hillside streams.

Little evidence remains on which to base an accurate picture of these early gardens. Literary references are allusory and indirectly descriptive rather than specific and reliably accurate. The gardens of the Medina Azahara are in ruins. Those of the Alcazar at Seville have possibly been influenced in their design more by the gardens of the Italian Renaissance than by the Arab and Spanish tradition with which they are more often linked. The striking arched jets, so much associated with the Generalife, are a relatively recent addition to the Patio de la Acequia, which itself was rebuilt over an earlier garden of similar but somewhat different proportions; an existing inscription in this early garden dates construction to the beginning of the 14th century. However, from similar archaeological data and references, including Muslim gardens and courtyards outside Spain, as well as a few remaining in Andalusia itself that retain an

112 The Cuarto Dorado, or Golden Court, also known as the Court of the Mosque, at the Alhambra, Granada. In spite of its impression of unity, the dates range from the 13th century (the column capitals) to post-1492 (the painted ceilings).

element of the early spirit, it is possible to form a reasonable and fairly reliable impression of these very early designs.

Influences possibly came from Damascus, Mesopotamia and Iran. Similarities of climate encouraged similarities of form, and the importation into Spain of plants from the east is recorded. Certainly a symbolic use of water and a delight in scents were introduced from Iran, while the enclosed courtyard came from Egypt via North Africa. The early gardens in Spain reflected the Muslim traditions of science, geometry and order. The role played by nature was secondary, although the gardens were clearly adapted to the climate and terrain in which they were located. In fact, from the 8th century, the area covered by the Islamic expansion paralleled that ecological area best described as 'Mediterranean'.

As the Umayyad dynasty declined, and the Almohads came to power, the capital was transferred to Seville. Early in the 13th century, the Christians re-entered Andalusia, and, after the fall of Seville in the middle of that century, the beauty and splendour of Muslim Spain was confined to the Sultanate of Granada. Finally, at the end of the 15th century, Granada was taken by the Christians under Ferdinand and Isabella, and the Moors were expelled from Spain. Many went to North Africa. The Moorish garden and courtyard, originally acknowledging North Africa as a source, now returned to influence that area.

Yet part of the architectural heritage remained in Spain. Richly embroidered plaster work, arabesques and intricate geometrical patterns abounded. The quality of architectural ornament was outstanding, while the Islamic spirit of contemplation was still faithfully reflected. The day-to-day enjoyment of life encouraged by Muslim belief was also echoed in the design of the gardens, and from Spain the Islamic garden heritage spread to other parts of the world. The gardens created during this period extended to Sicily and along the southerns shores of the Mediterranean to Egypt and Lebanon. The vast majority of the earliest gardens have been lost, but their irrigation systems are sometimes still traceable, and in them we may recognize the concept of the gardens eventually built in Mughal India. Many quiet and cloistered patios containing fountains and pools, shaded by cypress and orange trees, may still be found in Andalusia; and several of the region's great gardens have been continuously maintained with varying degrees of authenticity to the present day.

Concept The form of the Islamic garden was determined not only by symbolism but also by climate and topography, and in Spain as in most of the Islamic world this meant the promotion of coolness, shade and seclusion. Maximum emphasis was placed on whatever water was available. Stone and marble fountains, pools and edging were carved, although three-dimensional sculpture was forbidden. The planting of fragrant vegetation was encouraged. Andalusian gardens, established by local rulers for the most part near towns, were urban in character, and were well tended. They were generally small; and even if large were divided into small linked enclosures; in this respect, Spanish gardens differed from those of Iran and India.

The layout of the garden was, as customary, strictly geometric, and defined by walls of masonry or hedge. This geometric quality was emphasized by the parterres, which for irrigation were often well below the level of the paths. One result was that the vegetation did not conflict with the architecture; another

88

was that, since it was primarily the tops of flowers that were seen, and it was at this level that one walked, the garden gave the impression of a floral carpet – a fascinating example of the interrelationship between two of the Islamic arts. In addition, there was nearly always a fountain, but in Spain there were no large pools of water.

On the flat sites of Seville and Cordova, gardens as well as courtyards were regarded as outdoor rooms, forming part of the total building concept. High walls of white stuccoed masonry cast a welcome shadow. These walls were complete with a tile coping, or alternatively were topped with parapets that lined a walk. Walls separating one part of the garden from another often had arched windows containing a grille (*reja*) through which the views were particularly attractive. Tiled seats occupied the sills, while walled niches held vases or basins. Frequently, the gardens were further divided by lower walls of hedge.

In Granada, gardens were set on the hillsides, giving a lovely aspect. In fact, Granada was described by Arab historians as 'a goblet full of emeralds'. However, unlike the Mughal gardens in Kashmir, an area with which Andalusia shares some qualities of climate and terrain, hillside gardens in this area were slightly irregular. In this respect they were almost unique, and the unexpected interrelationships of the gardens of the Alhambra, or the quite exceptional curve of Velez Benaudalla, convey a charm and interest particular to the gardens of this province. A hillside location clearly gave more scope for variation and individual detail. Not only could it provide enclosed courts, but a view of the nearby town or city could be seen through a pierced wall or from an open terrace. Brick or tile staircases would connect various levels and, in contrast to Islamic gardens elsewhere, were more the result of necessity than a means to achieve visual drama. However, although the location of a staircase did not play a significant role in the overall design, it was treated in an attractive manner. Flights of steps were often sheltered by pergolas and lined with potted plants. Sometimes they were covered with bright tiles in geometrical patterns, and formed an effective contrast with the surrounding white stucco walls. Falling terrain also provided great scope for the arrangement of water and its distribution, and following a very ancient and sometimes spectacular tradition in the Mediterranean region, terraces were provided. Invariably, the Islamic garden in Spain was neatly ordered and fundamentally simple to build and maintain.

A distinctive feature of the Spanish garden was the small bower (*glorieta*). Derived from the Persian pavilion, and symbolizing the pearl pavilion of the Quranic paradise, it was located at the junction of paths. Often it was formed of cypress trees, the tops of which would be bent or clipped to form arches; alternatively, a light arch might be built and covered with vine.

Against the white stucco wall of the Spanish garden, green foliage was the predominant colour, followed by the purple-blue of the iris (*azul*), a colour taken up in the tiles. More prominent than flowers, but most effective when used sparingly, tiles faced benches and pools, paved walks, formed a circular base to trees, edged steps and flower beds and capped walls. Smooth glazed polychrome tiles were combined with more sombre unglazed tiles. As in western Asia, early tiles were cut into small geometric shapes from slabs of solid colour and fitted together as mosaic; subsequent techniques permitted more than one colour to be fired on the same tile without running together, and a raised line to be formed on the surface by the use of a metal matrix. The art form declined in the 16th century, when painted tiles were introduced.

Accessories such as benches, pots and fountains were carefully placed in the Spanish garden for maximum effect. Benches were often solid, standing on their own or else attached to a wall, with an inset tile backing. Unglazed tiles often formed walkways, sometimes laid in basket-weave pattern with a small coloured inset. Paths as well as steps were also faced with tiles, bricks, coloured earth or smooth pebbles laid in geometric patterns and ranging in colour from deep purple through grey to white. It is possible, however, that these and similar details may be relatively recent additions.

In Spain, the fame and attractions of the royal gardens were equalled by the charm of the domestic courtyard. House and garden were interrelated, and in Granada the one term *carmen* covered both. A Cordovan text of the 11th century describes a beautiful courtyard of white marble, down the centre of which a channel flowed into a basin. There was a pavilion in the centre. A row of trees planted on each side gave ample shade, and flowers cast their fragrance on the breeze.

Each courtyard was a complete unit in itself. Prosperous dwellings often contained more than one patio. It was a logical response to the climate found in most of the Islamic world, and was prefigured in the Roman atrium and the enclosed Iranian garden. It was in the patio that a large proportion of family living took place, although guests were not usually entertained there. As a result of the emphasis of family privacy, the courtyard was either wholly surrounded by the building itself, or, if against the street, was placed behind a high blank wall. From the street, only an occasional wrought iron gateway broke the unadorned façade. From here, a protected but inviting glimpse of a patio with its small pool, fountain and vegetation was revealed.

Stone paving would be relieved by brightly coloured tiles and potted plants such as roses, geraniums and carnations. Leaves would trail from upper level balconies. A cypress, or small orange tree or palm tree would give scale and, reinforced by a surrounding arcade, some shade. The focus of each patio was water in the form of a small pool or trickling fountain, and this provided a welcome sound as well as a little additional coolness to the enclosure.

Water   As in other parts of the Islamic world, water was important for reasons so varied as agriculture, religious symbolism and enjoyment. But it was scarce, and the Moors introduced a system of irrigation based on underground reservoirs and small canals. Sometimes the immediate source of water from which the garden was fed was a tank. Located at the highest point of ground, it was subsequently made a focal point and elaborately treated. From this tank, water was led either through underground pipes or open tiled channels to further pools, fountains or jets within the garden, before eventually reaching a kitchen garden or fields at a lower level. Sometimes well-heads marked an underground cistern of rainwater rather than a spring, and patio basins were supplied from rainwater collected off the roof tiles or courtyard paving. In the gardens, small conduits served the trees and shrubs. In the Patios de los Naranjos in both Cordova and Seville, water is led by channel from tree to tree, and controlled by small wooden blocks inserted as necessary. Plants were watered along a depression made with the soil between the rows. Unfortunately, further detail is difficult to obtain since the Spanish Arab textbooks on agricultural techniques, together with other Islamic literature, were burnt by the returning Christians.

Fountains portraying animals were popular throughout many parts of the Islamic world. Traces of an animal fountain have been found in the Medina Azahara, but the most famous example is to be seen in the Court of the Lions at the Alhambra. Basins were often very shallow, in order to use little water, or even sunken, their jets rising just above the level of the path. These basins are seen best from a height, such as the window of an adjacent building, or from a promenade wall. Stone or marble basins were circular, or of star or octagonal formation, faceted to exploit the water which brimmed over the edges. Spouts were of delicately and intricately wrought iron. Tiles were also used, glistening under the sunlit water. Small jets sometimes played over tiled paths. Flowing smoothly in a narrow runnel under dark arches, water linked palace courtyards and chambers, cloisters and gardens. Made the central motif, all other elements of the garden related to it.

Planting   Evergreen rather than deciduous trees were planted in the Spanish garden. Citrus trees were most common, followed by cypress and magnolia. The low box, of a later date, lent itself to geometrical expression, and was planted in hedges and clumps, or singly. Orange trees go back to the earliest gardens, and were often planted in rows. In later gardens, the maze became popular, and was formed of clipped box, cypress, myrtle, juniper or holly, preference being given to aromatic plants. Date palms, pomegranates and grapevines were also planted. Trees such as cypress, palm or pine were often placed in the centre of a flower bed to afford shade.

Flowers were often chosen for fragrance. They were planted in pots where the least water was needed. As accents, they played a significant role in the courtyard but in the garden they rarely played a major part and were used sparingly. Vases of coloured glaze or pots of terracotta lined garden walks and parapets. Myrtle, jasmine, narcissus, violets, roses, lilies, marjoram, carnations and poppies are among the flowers recorded as found in the Arab Moorish gardens; there were many more. There were also vegetables, such as artichoke and eggplant, as well as fruit trees, such as cherry, pear, plum, mulberry, apple, fig and lemon, since little distinction seems to have been made between flower garden and orchard. There was no grass, but there was some ground cover, such as moss. Planting tended to be concentrated, since there was much paving, though a dense massed grouping of blooms in the modern fashion was unknown.

The comprehensive irrigation system devised by and maintained under the Moors fell into disuse when they were expelled from Spain. With the breakdown of this system, the Islamic gardens of the Iberian peninsula almost all decayed and died. Although restoration has sometimes not been too faithful, in southern Spain it is still possible to enjoy, as did the early Caliphs, a garden's murmuring water, the song of the birds, the scent of its flowers and the green of its leaves.

Medina Azahara Cordova

This court city was built in the 10th century by Abd-ar-Rahman III for the empire of Al-Andalus. On south-facing slopes about four miles north-west of Cordova, the site is sheltered from the north wind and contains many springs. Over an area of 120 hectares there are three terraces, which contained the palace, gardens and other buildings including a mosque. The complex was used as a summer residence for the Umayyads, but within a century the caliphate ended and Medina Azahara was sacked by the Berbers. Destruction and looting continued over successive centuries. The site became a place for Cordovans to walk to, and is now being partially restored.

Water was carried to the site over a long aqueduct and through a stone-vaulted tunnel. It crossed ravines and passed through mountains to the foothills of the Sierra Morena where the Medina Azahara was located. After supplying the complex, the water continued mainly underground to Cordova. The gardens contained many pools and fountains. A great reflecting pool fronted the palace. There were terraces of marble and walks of mosaic. The stone-paved principal road through the site was bordered by irrigation channels, which fed all parts of the garden as well as a large number of fountains. One fountain in a garden pavilion was reputed to have been of green marble inlaid with gold and precious stones. There were cypresses and laurels, roses, lilies and jasmine. Hedges of clipped box, bay and myrtle divided the gardens into many small rectilinear areas. There were also animals and birds. Once grand in scale, the complex is now desolate. The archaeological restoration currently being undertaken leaves untouched the area that once contained the gardens with their pavilions, pools, fountains and channels.

113   A view over the extensive site of Medina Azahara, near Cordova. The once flourishing court city has long been in ruins, and nothing now remains of its original gardens with their reflecting pools and gushing fountains.

**Patio de los Naranjos
(La Mezquita)
Cordova**

The large mosque with its forest of columns and horseshoe arches, is in good condition, and although consecrated for Christian worship in the 13th century, is still known as La Mezquita (the Mosque). The courtyard garden was laid out in the 10th century; one side is formed by the main building, the other three by free-standing walls which at one time possibly formed a cloister. The rows of orange trees link indoor and outdoor spaces by echoing the aisles of columns within the mosque, but with the blocking of doors and archways this was less apparent. The arches are now being reopened. Each tree is set in a circular depression linked by narrow brick-lined irrigation runnels, while tall palms wave overhead. The courtyard also contains pools and fountains; it has a quiet serenity, and still serves as a charming meeting-place for visitors and citizens.

Plan 3   The mosque at Cordova, with its garden, the Patio de los Naranjos (Court of the Oranges). Almost the whole Moorish complex remains intact. Entering through its ancient gate (A), the Puerta del Perdon, next to the old minaret, one finds oneself in the patio (D) with its fountains (C) and the huge mosque itself (B) opposite. The only major addition has been the building of the Christian cathedral (E) in the middle of the mosque.

114   Narrow channels link the recessed beds of the trees within this courtyard, a commonly used method of irrigation seen also in the Patio de los Naranjos at Seville (plate 42).

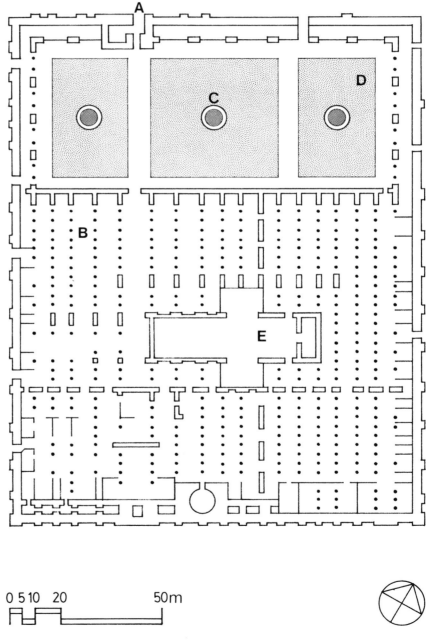

0 5 10 20   50m

115   Trees in the Patio de los Naranjos, the
Moorish Court of Ablutions to La Mezquita
at Cordova. The ends of the aisles within
the mosque were once partially open to the
courtyard, and the lines of trees seemingly
echoed the columns within.

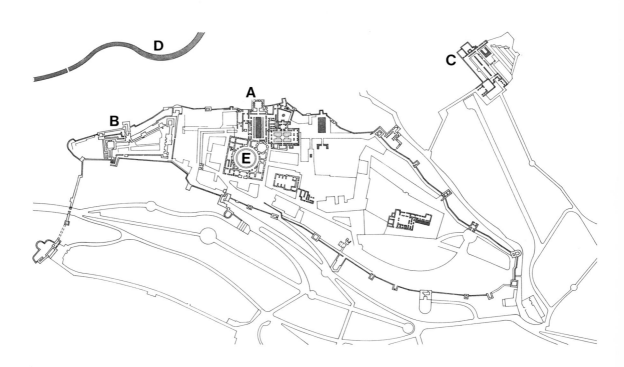

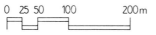

0 25 50   100   200m

**Alhambra
Granada**

A royal residence was established on the Alhambra plateau in the middle of the 13th century by Mohammed ben Al-Ahmar. Water was brought up from the River Darro. Considerable additions were made to the complex in the following century, but since the Alhambra, or Red Fort (Al Qal'a al-Hamra), was a fortress as well as a palace, the gardens were all contained within the ramparts. The buildings were restored and well maintained after Granada surrendered to Ferdinand and Isabella at the end of the 15th century. Charles V demolished some of them to make room for an intrusive and incongruous Italianate palace, but fortunately to a degree this may be ignored visually. The total effect of the red-orange buildings of the Alcazaba at the west end of the plateau and the Alhambra, with the treed, rocky slopes below and the snow-capped Sierra Nevada behind, is highly dramatic.

Leading inconspicuously from the Alhambra's main entry is the Court of the Myrtles (Patio de los Arrayanes) also known as the Court of the Pool (Patio de la Alberca). Its sunlit space is unexpected. At the north end is the warm amber glow of the Torre de Comares, its battlemented mass resting on a light arcade topped with carved plaster filigree. Behind the arcade is a dado of richly coloured *azulejos*. Down the centre of the court is a long rectangular pool, bordered by paths and two clipped myrtle hedges, and fed at each end by a low fountain in a flat basin. Goldfish swim in it; the still surface of the water is barely below the level of the paths and clearly mirrors the adjacent tower and arcade. To the south are similar arches and behind the hedges to the east and west are the two-storey wings of the Moorish palace, plain except for the elaborately carved stucco work surrounding the occasional door and window.

The Court of the Lions (Patio de los Leones) leads from the south-east corner of the Court of the Myrtles. In contrast to the latter's serenity, the decoration of the Court of the Lions is jewel-like in its richness. Narrowly spaced arches on a multiplicity of slender alabaster columns surround the court, and small square pavilions extend into the east and west ends of the enclosure. Gilded ceilings behind the arcades are

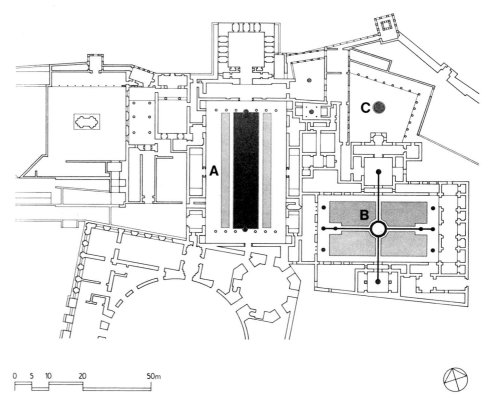

< Plan 4   Site plan of the Alhambra, with its attendant garden of the Generalife. The palace itself (A), with its many courts, lies behind a more heavily defended citadel, the Alcazaba (B). Generalife (C) was laid out as a summer retreat on a neighbouring hill, and both look out across the valley of the Darro (D). The palace of Charles V (E) impinges upon the Moorish work to the south.

Plan 5   The central complex of the Alhambra. The three main courts, round which the rooms are grouped with a mixture of symmetry and informality, are the Patio de los Arrayanes (A), the Patio de los Leones (B) and the Patio de Lindaraja (C). Charles V's palace intrudes at the bottom.

0   5   10   20   50m

116 A narrow runnel leads water from a fountain basin set in the floor of the Sala de Abencerrajes out to the central fountain in the adjacent Patio de los Leones, linking interior and exterior spaces.

117 Water bubbles into a low basin and flows into the central tank of the Patio de los Arrayanes (see general view, *below right*). Fishes were often to be found in the larger pools of Muslim courtyards and gardens, and are to be seen here as well as in the pool at Verinag (plate 194).

Below right
118 The Patio de los Arrayanes, in the Alhambra, Granada. The long channel of water leads the eye to a cool colonnade on the north side.

remarkable for their detailed stalactite carving. At the crossing of the two axes of the court is a fountain which discharges into a flat basin supported by twelve conventionally but simply carved lions; thin streams of water spout in a somewhat undignified manner from their mouths and run into a shallow surrounding channel. Very small additional fountains, which commence in the surrounding rooms, bubble into low basins on the axes of the central fountain, to which they are linked by narrow shallow runnels cut in the stone paving. The height of these fountains is related to that of people sitting down low. How densely the courtyard was once planted must remain a matter for conjecture. It is possible that its level was once a metre lower, so that the tops of flowers and flowering bushes would have been easily appreciated without the architecture being obscured. All the surrounding rooms are axially related to this court, in contrast to the seemingly casual relationship of one court to the other in the Alhambra as a whole.

The box and cypress planting of the Court of Daraxa (Lindaraja) is later in design. However, its raised basin is Arab, and light reflected from the Renaissance pool below plays on its scored and faceted under-surface.

The Alhambra is a remarkable Moorish achievement. Repairs and alterations have taken place over the course of time, and the early planting has considerably changed; but the interrelationship of its spaces, the proportions of its patios, the materials of its architecture and the assurance with which water was so effectively introduced have continued throughout succeeding centuries to afford the most profound satisfaction and delight.

96

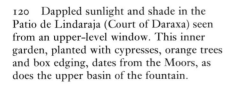

119 A portico surrounds the Patio de los Leones, and is articulated by two projecting pavilions at the east and west ends. The columns are short and thin, with ring-like mouldings and decorated caps and imposts. Note, too, the gradual transition from the closed room, through the connecting portico, to the open courtyard.

120 Dappled sunlight and shade in the Patio de Lindaraja (Court of Daraxa) seen from an upper-level window. This inner garden, planted with cypresses, orange trees and box edging, dates from the Moors, as does the upper basin of the fountain.

Generalife Granada

The Generalife was the summer residence of the Sultans of Granada. It was built for the Nazarite dynasty in the mid-13th century on a slope of the Cerro del Sol. The name is derived from 'garden of the architect' or 'of Arif' (Jennat al-Arif). It is composed of a series of small gardens, filled with planting and enlivened by water. At a higher level than the Alhambra and separated from it by a slight valley, the Generalife affords magnificent vistas over the city and countryside; the prospect is generally only appreciated from the windows and terraces, since the gardens themselves are enclosed and intimate.

The Court of the Long Pond (Patio de la Acequia) is the celebrated focus of the palace grounds. It is rectangular with porticoed pavilions at the north and south ends. These three-storey apartments have suffered from alteration and neglect, but they are sensitively scaled and partly obscured by foliage; they terminate the central canal's vista, but do not oppress the contained space. It is from these pavilions that the visitor obtains a primary view of the courtyard. A narrow aqueduct bordered by luxuriant flowers, trimmed myrtle hedges, orange trees and cypresses leads down the centre of the patio; the slender jets arching over it are of relatively recent date. The present level of the courtyard is fifty centimetres higher than that of the original but the *char bagh* of the plan is still apparent. To the west is an arcaded gallery with a small mosque at its centre; this gallery frames views of the Alhambra and the city. On the east there is a narrow service wing, behind which further gardens and terraces climb the hill. The north portico or lookout (*mirador*) provides a view of two other hills, the Albaicin and Sacromonte. Set low on the paving of both porticos is a lotus-shaped basin containing a small bubbling jet. The courtyard contains no polychrome mosaic, and, apart from the marble columns and plaster grillework of the pavilions, the predominant materials are stucco and clay tile.

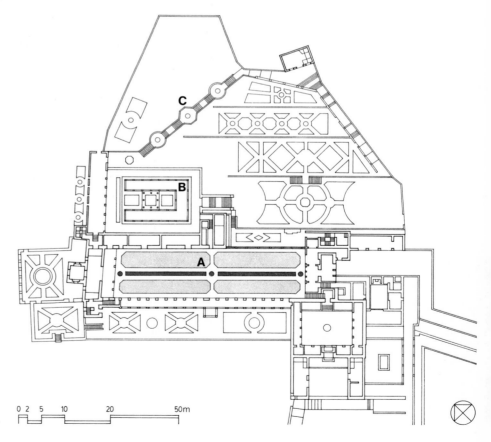

Plan 6   The garden of the Generalife, near the Alhambra, Granada. It is built on a steeply sloping site, the Patio de la Acequia (A) beneath the Patio de los Cipreses (B). Beyond are the steps and miniature waterfalls of the Camino de las Cascades (C).

0 2 5   10   20   50m

121 A view down the Patio de la Acequia of the Generalife at Granada. Seen through the portico at the north end of the garden is the entry pavilion.

122 One of three similar fountain basins in the main court. A slight depression in the surface of the paving catches any overspill, while coloured tile, set into the stone, creates a simple pattern.

Small gardens of later date, attractive in scale, lie a little higher up the slope to the east of the main courtyard. The Patio de los Cipreses is an enclosed garden with a U-shaped pool, numerous fountain jets and cypresses. Nearby is the Camino de las Cascades, which dates from at least the 16th century. Runnels of water flow down a channel on the top of its balustrade of rough masonry, and a small basin with a tiny jet rests in the centre of the stairs' three landings. The whole is shaded by dense foliage overhead.

Water is led into the Generalife from the higher reaches of the Darro. The pools and numerous fountains are an integral part of the garden's appeal, and the constant sound is an unfailing pleasure. Despite its superb setting and magnificent views, this Moorish garden remains a charming and intimately scaled representation of the paradise concept.

**Moorish Bath
Granada**

There is a small courtyard at the entrance to the remains of an 11th-century Moorish bath, its scale attractively domestic. Public baths (*hammam*) were found throughout the Islamic world, with rooms for cold, warm and hot water, possibly following Roman tradition. A characteristic of the *hammam* was that daylight penetrated through glass inserts set into a domed roof, and these domes contributed to the distinctive skyline of the Muslim city. The ablution basin in the mosque courtyard and the baths bear testimony to the importance of water and cleanliness in the hot and dusty Muslim world.

123 Planting dominates the courtyard at the entry to the Moorish Bath at Granada. Despite the ready water inside and the small area available for this courtyard, opportunity was still found to create a pool, just visible at the foot of the illustration.

Palacio de Daralhorra Granada

This domestic palace, with porticos on its north and south sides, upper-floor gallery, fountain with circular basin set into a hexagonal frame, leading into a simple rectangular pool, and pebble paving set in a diamond pattern, is very characteristic of the Moorish influence in Spain. At the beginning of the 16th century, this building was ceded to a convent, but the Moorish atmosphere remains. The main room of the residence affords views both in to the palace and out to the surrounding countryside, a panorama that includes the Albaicin, the Alhambra and the Sierra Nevada.

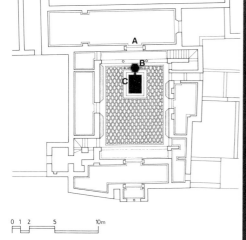

Plan 7   The Palacio de Daralhorra at Granada has many features in common with the Alhambra, though on a smaller scale: the portico (A) at the end of an open courtyard, and a basin (B) bringing water to a larger pool (C).

124   A view of the courtyard of the Palacio de Daralhorra at Granada. In the foreground is the courtyard's small basin and pool, surrounded by pebble paving set in a diamond pattern. We are looking from the top of the plan to the open landscape outside the window.

Velez Benaudalla near Granada

This early garden, in a village a few miles from Granada, was maintained until the Spanish Civil War, but it is now in poor condition and overgrown. The site's steep gradient has resulted in a uniquely asymmetrical layout, with the axis of the watercourse following the curve of a contour. There were once several gravity-fed fountains, located lower than the central canal. The garden contains an orchard as well as a decorative area, now in disuse, but restoration would still be possible.

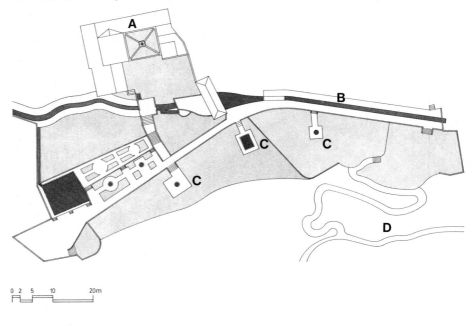

Plan 8   Velez Benaudalla, near Granada, is a house (A) overlooking a garden on a steep gradient. Its watercourse (B) once fed several fountains at a lower level (C) and the land then sloped down sharply to the valley (D).

Alcazar Seville

The Alcazar was the palace of the Moorish kings of Seville. The original 12th-century building was destroyed, but it was rebuilt in the 14th century by Moorish architects and craftsmen. The Alcazar garden is the largest in Spain that retains the Moorish tradition.

Within the palace there are several serene and attractively designed courtyards. These are surrounded by arcades, and in the centre is a low pool or basin which provides the sound and sparkle of water. Outside, the elements of the Alcazar garden are related to each other in an angular manner, and there are no vistas or alleys of trees. The garden has three divisions and is further divided into a series of small areas, the whole being enclosed by a wall. This wall, the raised paths, fountains basins and glazed tiles retain the Muslim tradition, though in other respects the garden has been considerably altered.

There is no unified design. The north-east section contains a rectangular pool and is bordered by a long gallery, while adjacent to the palace is the Garden of Maria Padilla, its enclosures intimate, almost like outdoor rooms. Dividing walls contain gateways and are surmounted by promenades. The garden's centre section has eight, hedged divisions; the third section has a 16th-century pavilion and pool. Despite the flat site, the three sections are at different levels connected by tiled steps.

There are many fountains of varied design, some at the level of the path and some raised on pedestals. From each, a bubbling jet emerges with a pleasant peaceful sound. Low benches abound, and the intimate scale provides many enclosed views.

125 (*above*) A richly decorated arcade surrounds this courtyard
at the Alcazar, Seville. The glazed tile dado and carved stucco
above are fully in the Moorish tradition, though they were in fact
built for a Christian king by Moorish craftsmen.

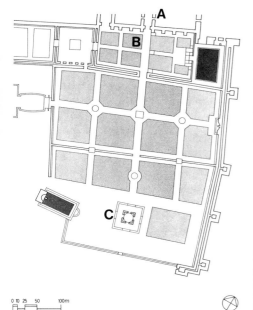

Polychrome tile (*azulejo*) is used on benches, steps, recessed window seats, fountains
and pools; paved surfaces are of brick or unglazed terracotta, often in herringbone or
basket-weave pattern, sometimes with a small coloured tile inset. The glazed tile is cool
in the heat, and provides colour when the flowering season is over. There are cypress,
palm, orange and lemon trees.

Although many original aspects of the garden have suffered through later additions
and alterations, there still remains a charm about the Alcazar's clipped hedges, stucco
walls, tall palms, tilework and glittering water; while the courtyards fully retain their
Moorish character.

0 10 25 50   100m

Plan 9   The Alcazar, Seville. From the
palace (A) one emerges into a typically
Moorish sequence of garden spaces (B). At
the further end is a pavilion (C) built by
Charles V.

Facing page

127 With no more than a single jet quietly pouring into a round stone basin set in the floor within the palace a marvellous effect is achieved.

128 A marble fountain-head set in a star-shaped pool with a glazed tile surround, the whole set at a crossing of brick pathways in the garden.

126 A simply carved fountain basin, floor recess and channel in another of the Alcazar's courtyards.

**Casa de Pilatos
Seville**

This late 15th-century mansion is an example of the Mudejar style, the term used to describe buildings executed for Christian clients by Muslim artists and craftsmen who remained in Spain following the reconquest; it displays Moorish, Gothic and Renaissance influences. There are many *azulejos*, both inside and outside. In the courtyard is a graceful arcade with marble columns. The garden contains a variety of planting.

129   A view of the courtyard of the Casa de Pilatos at Seville. Primarily of Mudejar style (i.e. produced for Christian patrons by Moorish craftsmen), it displays a curious mixture of Gothic and Renaissance influence as well as Moorish.

130 Sunlight and shadow in the garden of the Casa de Pilatos. There is a variety of planting, but Moorish influence has all but disappeared.

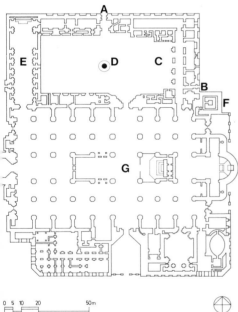

Plan 10 The Patio de los Naranjos, Seville. Entered by the Puerto del Perdòn (A) and the Puerto del Oriente (B), the patio (C) has a fountain (D) in the centre and is bounded by the sacristy (E) on the west. The old minaret, the Giralda (F), now serves as the campanile of the cathedral (G), whose huge bulk occupies the site of the mosque.

131 Fountain used for ablutions in the Patio de los Naranjos, Seville. Channels within the brick paving irrigate the orange trees, as at Granada.

Patio de los Naranjos   Seville

Dating from the 10th century, this patio adjacent to the old mosque contains orange trees set in strict formation. In the centre of the courtyard is a large circular fountain at which ablutions were performed. Water from this fountain fills channels linking the square beds at the base of each tree. The channels are now brick edged, but were once possibly stone lined. Their rectilinear geometry cuts across the diagonal pattern of the brick paving, while, in contrast, dappled shadows from the leaves overhead fall over all.

Safavid Iran

MOST OF IRAN is predominantly located at an altitude of more than one thousand metres. Its major area consists of the central plateau, bounded by the Elburz chain to the north and the Zagros mountains to the south. A large part of this area is uninhabited, and for the most part people live in the foothills and valleys, and along the coast. The air is clear and clean. The summers are very hot and dry and sometimes accompanied by a strong wind; the Caspian coastal areas are a little cooler. The winters are cold, although milder along the Caspian coast and the Gulf. The Caspian is below sea-level. Here, in contrast to the rest of the country, there is much rain, dense growth and intensive cultivation, and even the steeply pitched thatched roofs of dwellings look tropical. Several palaces, mansions and gardens overlooking the Caspian were built in this area; and since water was abundant, gardens contained many pools and channels. Elsewhere, vegetation is generally sparse, and although there is a short but beautiful spring in March and April, when many wild flowers appear, the creation of gardens is not easy. Everything must be irrigated.

Present-day Iran covers only a part of an empire that once extended well into Soviet Central Asia. Strategically located, Iran was in contact with and absorbed a variety of cultural influences; it also experienced many invasions. After the Medes and the Achaemenids, whose rulers included Cyrus, Darius and Xerxes, the Sassanian dynasty from Fars ruled the country. Conversion to Islam followed the Arab conquest in the 7th century, and the country was subsequently ruled by Abbasids, Seljuks, Mongols and Timurids. In the 16th century the Safavid dynasty was established and the country reached a peak under Shah Abbas at the turn of that century, when Isfahan was reputed to be one of the most beautiful cities in the world.

The major part of Iran has very little rain, and downpours are concentrated and sporadic. Evaporation is high, and porous ground encourages seepage. There are few year-round rivers. When wells were used, an ass or ox operated a treadmill, and the water was raised by scoop fixed to a belt between two wheels. There was also the *qanat* system. This method of water supply, which dated from Achaemenid times, drew upon the water table located at the base of the mountains, fed from melting winter snow. A master shaft, rarely exceeding 50 metres, was driven down to tap this source. From this point at regular distances along the route, which could be several miles long, vertical shafts were dug to a predetermined depth at an approximate spacing of 20–30 metres. These shafts followed a line leading to the location where the water was desired. Linking the base of these shafts, a slightly inclined tunnel of 1.5–2 metres in diameter was then dug. The shafts provided air for those building the tunnel as well as a means for the disposal of the excavated material. This perennial supply of water was stored in tanks or was directed into open channels at its destination. From there, by gravity, it flowed through gardens, worked fountains, turned the wheels of flour mills or watered crops, until every drop had been utilized.

132 The north-east corner of the courtyard of the Mader-i Shah Medersa, defined by the tiled and stuccoed two-storey arcade formed by the students' rooms; the whole composition is reflected in the still waters of the pool.

109

Concept　Surrounded by miles of exposed, sun-baked land on the wind-swept plateau, an oasis came to exemplify for the Muslim an image of paradise, with its green, shaded garden, and the sound of trickling water. Recalling the biblical Garden of Eden, such a paradise was a natural reward for the faithful. Besides, the royal pleasure garden had already existed in Iran in pre-Islamic times. These two traditions of the garden, one sacred, one secular, each influenced the other, and the sweet-scented garden of the Quran, with its many flowers and trees was often compared to its earthly counterparts.

Few if any Iranian gardens remain that date back more than five hundred years; however, those designed more recently in the Islamic tradition seem compatible with earlier records, miniatures and the main features symbolically depicted on garden carpets. There are a number of elements consistently found in these gardens. Water, in a centrally placed pool, was essential for irrigation and also cooled and moistened the air. From the pool, clearly defined canals stretched out along the garden's length, and often across it. Flowers such as roses gave colour and scent. Trees bore fruit or simply provided shade, such as plane and cypress. Sound was created by the trickling water of fountains and the song of birds, as well as by conversation and song accompanied by stringed instruments.

Garden art is transitory, continuously subject to growth, the whims of successive owners and gardeners and the chance of decline. Nonetheless, through descriptions and other records, it is possible to recreate some early concepts, while discounting possible hyperbole. Accounts exist of the Achaemenid garden, and the Sassanian garden plan has also been traced. Records were made more than 2,500 years ago of gardens planted by Cyrus the Great. These were probably orchards, as the trees were set out in straight lines. The application of symmetry, the *char bagh* and use of defining water courses, avenues, the closure of vistas, terraces and kiosks, existed long before Islamic times. The courtyard was an ancient concept; the garden was out of place in an urban centre, and evidence of courtyards has been found in Achaemenid dwellings and Parthian and Sassanian palaces.

A basic, if somewhat deprecatory, description of the Iranian Islamic garden was given by Sir John Chardin, an Anglo-French jeweller who travelled through that part of the world in the 17th century:

> The Garden of the Persians commonly consist of one great Walk, which parts the Garden, and runs on in a straight line, border'd on each side by a Row of Plantanes, with a Bason of Water in the middle of it, made proportionable in Bigness to the Garden, and likewise of two other little Side-Walks, the Space between them is confusedly set with Flowers, and planted with Fruit-Trees, and Rose-Bushes; and these are all the Decorations they have.

A description by some travellers one and a half centuries later gives a little more flavour:

> Of these gardens we ventured to enter one, which was renowned all over the country for its beauty and fruitfulness . . . It consists of a fine alley of chenar trees, which leads up to a pleasure house . . . built on the elevation of six terraces, from each of which falls a beautiful cascade conducted by Kanauts from the neighbouring mountains. On the right and left is a wood of fruit trees of every sort and description, with a fine crop of grass at their roots. From the pleasure house is seen, through the alleys of chenars, the whole territory of Kho, one of the most lively landscapes that we found in Persia.

Such a garden is not an isolated occurrence. A further early 17th-century description by Sir Thomas Herbert, who was with the British embassy in Iran, relates to an impression of Isfahan:

> Gardens here for grandeur and fragour are such as no City in Asia out-vies; which at a little distance from the City you would judge a Forest, it is so large; but withal so sweet and verdant that you may call it another Paradise; and Agreeable to the old report, *Horti Persarum erant amoenissimi*. At the West end of Spahawn is that which is called Nazer-Jereeb; A Garden deservedly famous. From the Mydan if you go to this Garden you pass by Cherbaugh, through an even Street near two miles long, and as broad as Holborn in London, a great part of the way being Garden-walls on either side the street; yet here and there bestrew'd with Mohols or Summer-houses; all along planted with broad-spreading Chenaer trees, which besides shade serves for use and ornament. Being come to the Garden (or rather fruit-Forest) of Nazer-Jereeb, you find it circled with a high wall which is about three miles in compass, entered by three Gates that are wide and well built. From North to South it was a thousand of my paces; from East to West seven hundred; and the prospect from one end to the other easily and fully discovered, by reason there is a fair open Ile (like that in Fountainebleau) which runs along, and is formed into nine easie ascents, each surmounting or rising above the other about a foot, all being very smooth and even. In the center or middle of the Garden is a spacious Tank, formed into twelve equal sides, each side being five foot, set round with pipes of lead, which spout the liquid element in variety of conceits: and that sort of pastime continues to the North Gate, where is raised a pile for prospect and other sort of pleasure, antickly garnished without, and within divided into six rooms. The lower part is adorned with Tanks of white Marble, which fume out a cool breeze by quaffing so much crystalline water as makes it bubble there by a constrained motion; the Aquaduct being brought by extraordinary charge and toil thither from the Coronian Mountain.

The garden as a theme was repeatedly found in many of the arts of Iran, and the depiction of nature lent itself to a stylized elaboration that was remarkable in its own right. Painted miniatures flourished in the 15th and 16th centuries, often illustrating legends and princely pursuits. The setting for many of these was the garden, showing kiosks, pools, water channels, fountains, trees and flowers, all carefully delineated. Affairs of state, lovers, feasts and entertainments were all depicted in this setting. Atmosphere and activity at a particular moment were clearly conveyed, although the relationship of these details to the overall composition or plan was not always revealed. Unfortunately, by the late 17th century, the original and characteristic stylization had given place to the desire for correct representation, and, as commonly happens, an era of decline began.

Carpets carried geometric stylizations of garden plans and often depicted a *char bagh*. They showed pools and intersecting water channels, often containing fish. Trees were usually cypress, possibly since this was the easiest to represent, with birds among the foliage. Flowers and shrubs grew in rectangular beds and also helped fill the available space. These carpets were richly designed and colourful, reflecting delight in the garden itself, while they softened the effect of the tile or stone floors and bare walls of the rooms in which they were placed.

Miniatures and carpets were the chief vehicles for the portrayal of garden art; there were also albums of flower paintings, as well as flowers and gardens on pottery, fabrics, book covers, metalware and faience. The garden theme also constantly occurred in poetry. Iran was often described as the 'Land of Poets and Gardens'. The garden was praised for itself and was used as the setting for many narratives, while the beloved was likened to a rose, jasmine or cypress.

Firdausi's *Shahnama* is devoted to gardens and their flowers; Sadi's *Rose Garden* (*Gulistan*) is modelled on the paradise of the Quran, in that the structure of the poem is deliberately divided into eight parts; and Hafez sang the praises of the gardens of Shiraz, where he and Sadi are buried. Omar Khayyam of Khorasan, who regretted 'that Spring should vanish with the rose', desired to be laid to rest in a spot upon which the wind would scatter blossoms.

The practical use of gardens varied. Primarily, a garden was enjoyed for the welcome relief it provided against the hot sun of the plains, its vegetation a contrast to aridity outside. Trees provided shade, while water cooled the air and refreshed the body. It was an oasis of quiet, where the beauty of the plants and water could be admired. It was common practice for a prosperous Iranian to own a garden outside the city, to which he and his family retreated for several days at a time during the heat of the summer. The Iranian garden was a place in which to admire the view and breathe fresh air – to occupy, rather than merely walk through as would a European. Sir John Chardin noted that, 'the Persians don't walk so much in Gardens as we do, but content themselves with a bare Prospect, and breathing the fresh Air: For this End, they set themselves down in some part of the Garden, at their first coming in to it, and never move from their Seats till they are going out of it.'

When their presence was not required elsewhere, rulers spent a major part of their time in the garden, conducting affairs of state as well as indulging in less serious pursuits. Fine carpets, silk cushions, rich awnings, tents, singers and musicians helped create the setting for royal magnificence. Even when travelling, rest and diversion were taken along the route in gardens located there for such a purpose.

In fact, the garden played a major role in the lives of many people in Iran. Holidays were spent there, and it was the scene of celebration and entertainment to which one went with the company of friends for lively discourse, to eat refreshments and to listen to music. A traveller in Shiraz in the 17th century even recounted that he saw 'ropes or cords stretched from tree to tree in several gardens, Boys and Girls and sometimes those of riper years swinging upon them'.

More often the garden served as a private place. It was a quiet retreat, where flowers, trees and water could be fully appreciated and enjoyed. Surrounded by walls, it provided a setting for quiet meditation and reflection. Students and teachers met there to study and debate. The garden was the setting for the determination of ministerial policy, or for the concluding of business contracts. The garden filled a great variety of purposes and played a fundamental role in the Iranian way of life.

Since the garden was usually private, the personal ideas and preferences of owner and designer were clearly visible. Nonetheless, there were features common to every Iranian garden. The typical layout, found at least as early as the Sassanian period, was the *char bagh*, or quartered garden. In a large garden the segments would be further subdivided, either by a series of brick or flagstone paths parallel to both axes equally, or more frequently by emphasizing the longitudinal axis, with minor paths echoing the transverse. Main axes were formed by canals and long avenues, minor axes by straight paths; intersections were often marked by a pool or pavilion. Further locations for pavilions were on two or four sides of the garden, where they made a focal point. Located on an axis, and providing additional shade, a pavilion served as a viewing platform from which the water, trees and flowers could be enjoyed.

Sometimes rugs were placed under coloured tents or awnings, but generally in the Iranian garden the shelter was more permanent, with a decorative roof supported on poles sheltering a balustraded platform. Such pavilions, often depicted in miniatures, were sometimes brightly coloured elaborate structures of two storeys.

To afford protection from the outside world, and to ensure privacy, the garden was surrounded by a high wall. Often built of mud brick, it was quite plain, although the walls surrounding some of the royal gardens were embellished with towers. Miniatures portrayed battlements echoing those of the city wall; and wrought-iron finials, paintwork and tiles were also seen. Appropriately enough, many walls carried trellises for climbing plants. Between them, side pavilions and surrounding walls gave a sense of enclosure to the garden similar to that of the courtyard, although on a different scale.

Water   Irrigation was indispensable, and the canals of the garden echoed the systems used for watering crops. A geometric layout was commonly used for the canals, even on gradients. Straight canals defined areas of grass and planting. With great economy of means, the water in these gardens played more than a mere functional role. Dark deep tanks and tiled basins, flowing channels, thrusting jets and splashing cascades all added to the attraction.

Water was appreciated in many different ways. In pools, its dark reflecting quality was preferred, whereas in channels, its movement and clarity were emphasized by blue tiles. The pleasant noise of water was enjoyed when it gurgled through runnels, or was broken up by a chute. When motionless, the glossy sheen provided a textural contrast as well as a mirror to the varied foliage. Petals of roses or other flowers were strewn on the water's surface, and apples were placed on the top of fountain sprays, or set to float on the pool below.

Pools were found in the gardens of the rich, and in the courtyards of the urban dweller. They were filled from storage tanks – from which they were drawn – or from open channels, which in the city flowed down streets and lanes. In gardens they served as reservoirs, and in mosques they were used for ablutions. The sides of the pool were built above the surrounding ground, and there was a peripheral gutter to take the overflow. This gutter was necessary since, in order to appear shimmering and unconfined, the pool was filled to its brim, the edges were precisely levelled and water flowed over on every side. When filled to its edge, the scale of the pool seemed larger. Reflection and reality merged, and because there was no coping to cause disruption it supplied a striking symbolic representation of image on substance, of heaven on earth.

Pools varied in size from the large straight-sided 'little seas' (*daryaches*) to very small basins. Often they contained a single fountain, sometimes a number of jets. There was also a great range of shape, although always geometrical and never freely formed. Most frequent was the rectangular tank, but square, octagonal, circular, lobed and cross-shaped tanks were also found. Sometimes a pool would be located within a pavilion, where it would clearly reflect the elaborate ceiling.

Although multiple jets and a wide variety of nozzles may have been unknown, great use was made of water pressure, and patterns were made by opening and closing individual valves. Fed by lead pipes, jets were located both indoors and out, contributing both form and delightful sound.

Planting   Shade trees formed a major feature in the Iranian garden, and large numbers of sycamore and plane were planted to cast their shadow over water, against walls and over paths, which were therefore narrow. Other trees frequently found were the poplar, used for building since it grew quickly, and the cypress, appreciated by poets as a symbol of eternity and death, since it did not rejuvenate after being cut. In contrast, the delicate rosy sprays of the almond or silver flowering plum were emblems of life and hope. Elm, ash, pine, oak, maple, spruce and willow together with hawthorn and myrtle bushes were also found in the Iranian garden. Trees were regularly planted in rows, one particular species at a time being used to border an avenue or define or fill a distinct section. Trees were very highly regarded and Shah Abbas is reputed to have planted gold and silver coins among the roots to assist their growth. Occasionally flowers, but more usually grass, extended to the base of the trunk, very different from the circular bed commonly found in Andalusia.

Fruit trees were prized not only for what they produced but also for their decorative qualities. Of the fruit trees that were planted in the Iranian garden – apple, apricot, mulberry, cherry, fig, lime, orange, lemon, peach, melon, pear, plum, pomegranate, grapes and quince were among them – many were appreciated for their blossom. On walls and pergolas grew the grapevine, since the Quran's strictures against wine were not always interpreted too strictly. Nuts, such as the almond, hazelnut, pistachio and walnut, were also grown.

Flowers, depicted or referred to with possible ceremonial significance in Achaemenid and Sassanian times, offered colour and fragrance. New plants – vegetables, fruit and anything exotic – were always welcomed. Such gifts were brought to the Shah from Europe, as well as from other parts of Asia.

Not many flowers were named in early works on gardening, but from poetry, carpet designs and pottery it was possible to discover which flowers were grown. Firdausi's *Shahnama* is such a source. Often mentioned, and therefore presumably widely grown, were lilacs, lilies and roses. Irises, marigolds and, especially in Isfahan, jonquils and tulips were grown in Iran for many centuries. Also common were jasmine, narcissus, anemones, carnations, crown imperials, cyclamen, daffodils, hollyhocks, hyacinths, violets, larkspur and poppies.

Pride of place went to the rose. Planted informally, or massed in bowers, it was universally popular and even formed the subject of festivals. Praised by poets, it provided a popular theme. Hafez, describing the Persian spring, wrote, 'Earth rivals the Immortal Garden during the rose and lily's reign', and the beloved was often compared to a rose. The word for rose was *gul*; it was also used as a generic term for flower, and as such is also found as a compound word, such as *gul-i-marges* (narcissus). Colours ranged from amber and orange through to yellow and white, with all shades of red, and many combinations. Garden plants were appreciated in their original form, or were improved by selective breeding rather than through cultivation of hybrids. The Iranians remained as conservative in their attitude to plants as in their approach to architecture.

All flowers were precious, especially since in the hot, dry climate the blooming season was so short. Contemporary miniatures show the disposition of flowers in the Iranian garden. Flowers were planted in mass display for their scent as well as colour (rose-water was used as perfume), and were also set out individually or in informal groups among the sparse grass, sometimes, with the exception of roses, under trees. The few parterres evident in the Iranian garden were probably of European influence, and there were no regular rows or herbaceous borders. A 14th-century description of narcissus meadows near Kazarun and Jirra in Fars, describes the grass as 'all full of self-sown narcissus, so that all the plain is covered with flowers. It is most famous, and such is the sweet smell of the narcissus in these meadows, that, while it goes to the head, the heart is rejoiced thereby.'

Also playing a decorative role in the gardens were animals and birds. Gazelles and peacocks roamed under the trees in the larger gardens, nightingales sang above, pools contained fish, or were a home for swans, pelicans and ducks. In some of the royal gardens, there were zoos and aviaries; the ancient tradition of hunting was carried out on the periphery.

Notwithstanding the natural beauty of the trees, flowers, fruit, water, birds and animals, and the sounds and fragrances that were so much a part of the Iranian garden, bright artificial plants were created for winter, when the real garden was barren. Such a tradition was old. A report of trees of gold and grapevines of precious stones dates from the Achaemenid period, and a famous garden carpet of metal thread and jewels is told of in Sassanian times. Many centuries later, in the *Shahnama*, Firdausi described an artificial tree of silver, gold and jewels, its hollow fruits filled with wine, and there were several subsequent reports of royally owned jewelled trees. If these accounts were true, and there is little reason to doubt their substance, even allowing for some exaggeration it is possible that such products of the jeweller's art must have been not only luxurious but somewhat startling, their beauty questionable by today's tastes. For the less wealthy there were miniature gardens of painted wax, as well as of paper and paste. For some, the materials were luxurious, for others, commonly available and cheap; for all Iranians, the love of gardens was constant and pervasive.

**General Plan
Isfahan**

Isfahan grew as a city in response to its inhabitants' needs. It was then adopted by the monarch as his capital, when new avenues and a number of monuments were created. Many green areas were laid out by the Safavids, each formally defined and following the *char bagh* pattern. They reflected the Islamic attitude to art as a whole in that they could be added to indefinitely without attempting a finality, which was the prerogative of Allah.

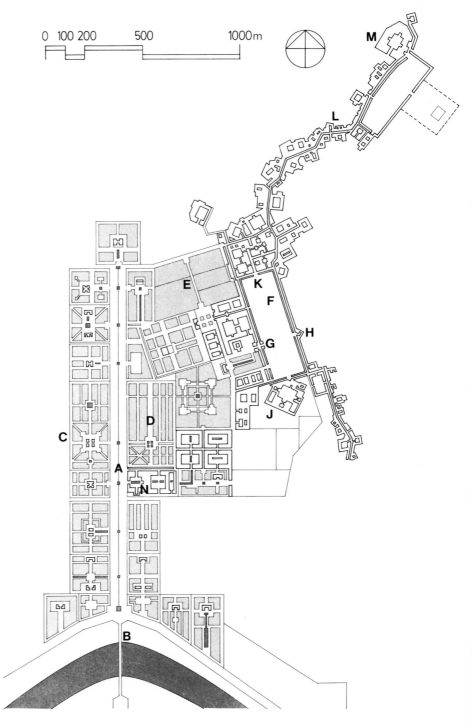

Plan 11 The modern city of Isfahan is built on what was a series of palaces and gardens. Its central spine is the Char Bagh Avenue (A) leading to the Bridge of Allahverdikhan (B). The other main features are as follows: C, Gardens of the Vazirs; D, Hasht Behesht; E, Chehel Sutun; F, Maydan; G, Ali Qapu; H, Masjid-i Shaykh Lutfullah; J, Masjid-i Shah; K, Bazaar gateway; L, Bazaar; M, Masjid-i Jami; N, Mader-i Shah Medersa.

Many of the main features of the city plan were established by the mid-17th century: Char Bagh Avenue, running north to south, which crosses the Zayandeh-Rud River over the Bridge of Allahverdikhan; the Gardens of the Vazirs to the west; and the palace gardens, including the Chehel Sutun, to the east. The long rectangle of the Maydan is clearly visible, with the Ali Qapu on its west side, the Masjid-i Shaykh Lutfullah on its east, and the Masjid-i Shah at an angle to the south. The bazaar complex begins to the north, leading to the Masjid-i Jami in the far north-east corner.

Ali Qapu
Isfahan

The Ali Qapu was originally a monumental gateway on the west side of the Maydan. It was built by Shah Abbas in the early 17th century, and received subsequent additions from his successors. It led to other pavilions, stables, royal storehouses, workshops, housing many precious articles and foodstuffs, and the harem. This vast complex extended between the Maydan and Char Bagh Avenue, set amidst woods, pools, fountains and channels of running water. The area was restricted to nobles, royal guests, servants and guards; its character has long since changed, and it is now largely built over.

133 The Ali Qapu, Isfahan, seen across the Maydan. It was once the gateway to a vast complex of royal buildings and gardens that extended behind it westward to Char Bagh Avenue.

It was the Ali Qapu that was the point of contact between the palace and the outside world. Here there was a throne room, apartments for the Shah and rooms for entertainment and reception. On the large terrace overlooking the Maydan, the Shah entertained guests and observed the city skyline as well as activities taking place in the Maydan, including polo games. The roof of the porch is supported by eighteen slender columns. On the floor of the porch is a lead-lined marble basin, where once three fountains played, supplied with water that had been raised by oxen to an upper level. Now the pleasures of the view, as well as of the building itself, are shared by numerous visitors.

134   A corner of the marble basin on the floor of the porch from which the Shah and his guests overlooked the Maydan. On the right is the foot of one of the wooden columns supporting the roof.

135   An overflow drain carved in the marble edge of the basin set in the floor of the porch of the Ali Qapu, typical of the aesthetic care devoted to every functional element.

Char Bagh Avenue Isfahan

Located west of the palace area, this avenue is now a main traffic artery, although it was built to serve as a promenade. It runs at a slight gradient for about a mile down to the Zayandeh-Rud River, where it is continued by the 17th-century Bridge of Allahverdikhan to the opposite bank, which at one time contained further royal gardens.

Originally, the avenue was lined with palatial apartments and kiosks with gardens behind. It was over fifty metres wide, and contained a canal down its centre, which cascaded from successive terraces and was bordered with wide stone paving. The avenue was framed by poplars and several rows of plane trees, many of which were cut down at the end of the last century. There were tanks of various sizes and shapes, and many fountains. Today the wide avenue remains, but it is somewhat ordinary, commercial in character and a major route for dense traffic.

136   A view to the north along Char Bagh Avenue, Isfahan. Today, although the tree-lined central strip is for the pleasure of pedestrians, the central canal has disappeared, and heavy traffic, some of which may be seen through the trees, flows on each side.

Chehel Sutun Isfahan

Part of this royal pavilion may have been built, and its garden laid out, as early as the end of the 16th century. The pavilion was extended by Shah Abbas II in the 17th century, and repaired after fire at the beginning of the 18th century. The indoor space of the pavilion and the outside garden are completely interrelated. The great porch, with its painted wood mosaic ceiling inlaid with mirrors, overlooks a long reflecting pool. In the centre of the porch, supported by slender fluted cedar columns, is a white marble basin into which four carved lions spouted water. A throne used to be located at the rear of the porch, behind which is a banqueting hall containing large oil paintings. The garden, which originally had more than one pool, several fountains and additional entry pavilions, has undergone several changes since it was first designed, but the grand pool remains, and there are extensive areas of grass, well treed.

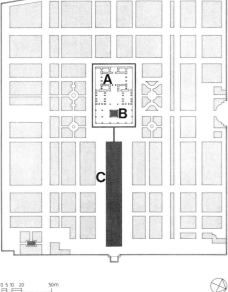

0 5 10 20   50m

Plan 12　Chehel Sutun, Isfahan. The pavilion (A) lies open to the garden. In front of it stands a basin (B) leading to a long pool (C). The garden extends on all sides in symmetrical parterres though it has been altered since Safavid times.

137　The north-east corner of the Chehel Sutun at Isfahan. Slender wooden columns support the roof of the great porch, which, on its platform, overlooks the length of the garden. It was badly damaged at the time of the Afghan occupation and has suffered periods of neglect since then, but some restoration has recently taken place.

138 Carved stone bases at the foot of the fluted cedar columns. In the centre of the platform is a large rectangular marble basin that was once filled by fountain jets and by water spouting from the carved lions.

Mader-i Shah Medersa Isfahan

The theological college (*medersa* or *madrassa*) of the Mother of the Shah (Mader-i Shah), built at the beginning of the 18th century, is entered off busy Char Bagh Avenue. Its impressive tile and marble entry portal contains doors with gilt medallions, and is decorated with intricate arabesques of white flowers on an ultramarine background above the marble and tile frieze. Inside, the two-storey arcades of this late Safavid masterpiece enclose a tranquil courtyard, around which 150 students used its various rooms for living, study and meditation. A long canal at the foot of steps that stretch its length links the entry portico with the *iwan* at the east end, and to the side there is an additional ablution pool, filled to the brim with dark water. Large plane trees, as old as the building itself, cast a varied pattern of light and shade across the courtyard.

Plan 13 The Mader-i Shah Medersa. Bounded by a bazaar at one side (A) and Char Bagh Avenue in the front where the entrance is placed (B), the *medersa* consists essentially of four wings with the sanctuary (C) in the centre of one of them. A long canal (D) bisects the courtyard (E).

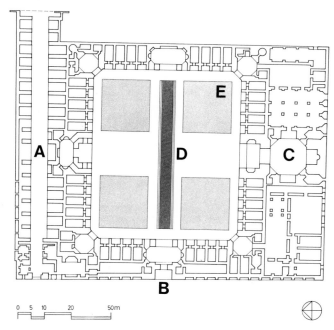

Facing page
139 A carved stone basin in the entry portico of the Mader-i Shah Medersa at Isfahan stands in silhouette against the garden beyond. Gilt medallions cover the door leading from Char Bagh Avenue, while multicoloured tilework and flowing calligraphy cover the opposite wall.

120

**Masjid-i Jami
Isfahan**

This mosque is a majestic monument of Seljuk architecture. Over successive centuries it has been expanded, and has suffered much damage as well as reconstruction; nevertheless, it remains one of the most significant buildings in the Islamic world. It is an urban mosque set behind high walls in an old part of the city, and is approached through a small fabric bazaar. The complex is grouped around a large rectangular stone-paved courtyard, in the centre of which stands an ablution pool. There is also a lobed pool and several raised basins. Surrounding the courtyard is a two-storey arcade faced with mosaic faience on buff brick. In the centre of each side is a deep *iwan*.

140   Lobed pool with basin beyond, silhouetted against an *iwan* in the courtyard of the Masjid-i Jami, Isfahan. A more extensive view of the courtyard of this large and ancient mosque may be seen in plate 61.

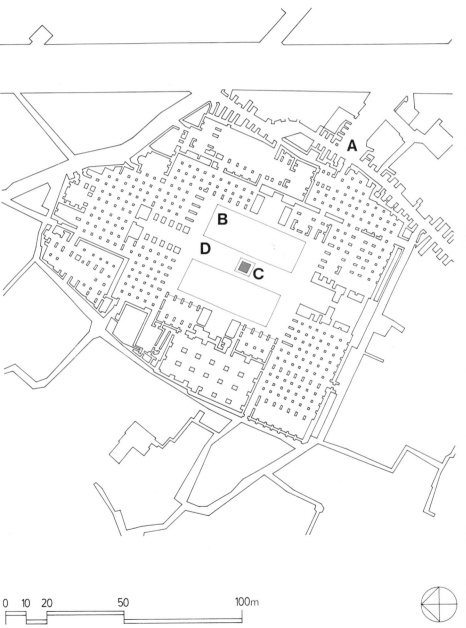

Plan 14   The Masjid-i Jami, showing how the mosque and its outbuildings are integrated into the fabric of the city. The entrance (A) is from the bazaar. From here one arrives at the courtyard (B) with its ablution fountain (C) and lobed pool (D) shown above.

0 10 20   50   100m

**Masjid-i Shah
Isfahan**

The Royal Mosque (Masjid-i Shah), built at the beginning of the 17th century, is a magnificent example of Safavid art. The grand entry portal completes the south end of the Maydan. With a scarcely perceptible turn to the right to acknowledge Mecca in the south-west, the entry leads to an inner stone-paved courtyard. This has an ablution basin in the centre, its dark water right to the brim. The design of the courtyard itself is simple, if not positively severe, but around it are four great *iwans* linked by two-storey arcades, while above are the high cupola of the main sanctuary and the flanking minarets. Rich mosaics of blue, turquoise and black cover most surfaces. Their intricate and interwoven stylized patterns, in a wealth of floral displays, reflect the Iranian passion for flowers, and at the same time symbolize the Muslim desire for the continuance of abundant life.

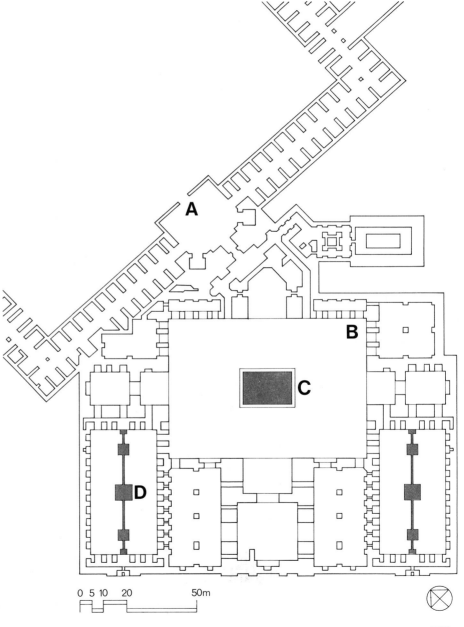

Plan 15   The Masjid-i Shah, Isfahan, opens off the great Maydan by an obliquely angled entrance (A) leading to the main courtyard (B) with its customary ablution pool (C) in the centre. Flanking the mosque are two smaller courtyards with water channels, one of them (D) a *medersa*.

0 5 10   20   50m

Facing page

141   The dome of the main sanctuary seen from the courtyard of the southern *medersa*. The dome's arabesques of yellow or sandalwood on a turquoise ground are separated from the high drum by a characteristic band of white calligraphy on a blue ground. The base of golden brickwork, which is almost unadorned, provides an effective contrast to the glazed dome and drum above.

142   The *iwan* in the centre of the north-west arcade of the Masjid-i Shah, reflected in the large rectangular basin for ablutions. Floral motifs predominate in the extensive tilework, although the decoration is richer on the south-west side, which faces Mecca.

Maydan Isfahan

143   A view across the Maydan at Isfahan from the porch of the Ali Qapu. The pattern of the grassed areas has changed over the years, but the continuous two-storey façade that encloses the square, and the total effect of its great scale remain. On the horizon in the centre of the illustration may be seen the dome and minarets of the Masjid-i Jami.

The Maydan, or 'Garden of the Plain', is one of the largest public squares in the world, and formed the centre of the town-planning activities of Shah Abbas I. To the north of the Maydan is the entry to Isfahan's great bazaar. At the opposite end is the Masjid-i Shah, and to the east and west respectively are the Masjid-i Shaykh Lutfullah and the Ali Qapu. A unifying two-storey façade of *iwan* niches surrounds this rectangular area; these once contained goldsmiths, metalworkers, druggists and cotton, wool and silk merchants. On market days a great variety of goods were on sale under temporary tents and awnings, and entertainers enlivened the scene. On other occasions the Maydan saw horsemanship, marksmanship and polo, played by the Shah and his courtiers. Today some of the trades and commercial activities remain around the perimeter, while the Maydan is surrounded by parked cars, and its grassed areas contain municipal planting. The grand scale of its space and its role in linking some of Safavid architecture's greatest monuments cannot be diminished.

Bagh-i Fin Kashan

Kashan is located near the arid Great Kavir, but the city receives its water supply from a spring and *qanats*. A few miles outside the town is the Bagh-i Fin. Although established in the 16th century by Shah Abbas I, the early buildings have disappeared. The present garden dates from the time of Fath Ali Shah at the beginning of the 19th century. Restoration work is slowly taking place. Within the walls is a small paradise. Walks are lined with plane and cypress trees, and flowers bloom in abundance. There is a constant flow of water into a pool in the far corner of the garden. This supplies a further pool, bordered by great trees, as well as several tiled channels. There are fountains galore: in the large pool, down the centre of several channels and in runnels along their border. With its shade, planting and constantly running water, this paradise garden is literally an oasis in the desert.

Plan 16   Bagh-i Fin, Kashan, a 19th-century garden following traditional lines. Enclosed in a continuous rampart, water enters close to one of the square pools (A), and has a pavilion (B) in the centre.

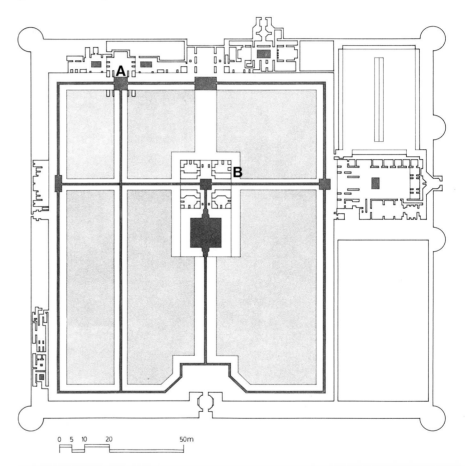

144   One of the tiled channels that run through the Bagh-i Fin. Fountains spout down the centre of the channels as well as in the central pool. The abundance of water in this garden, its many shade trees and its flowers together provide a high dramatic contrast to the surrounding desert.

126

Bazaar (segment) Kashan

Spatially the Iranian bazaar follows a linear route, which allows growth and change within an overall organization. Off the main paths are numerous small cells containing shops, with passageways at irregular intervals leading to larger spaces or courtyards. These courtyards are communal, contain pools and, frequently, are planted. Arcaded spaces may surround the courtyard, and sometimes there is a prayer *iwan* two storeys in height. In contrast to the bazaar passageways, which are often poorly lit, these courtyards are flooded with sunlight, and with their planting are delightful retreats from the tightly packed activities of the bazaar.

145 View of one of the sunlit courtyards reached by a passageway in the enclosed bazaar at Kashan. Used to store items intended for the bazaar, its pool and trees provide a quiet relief from the surrounding noise and bustle.

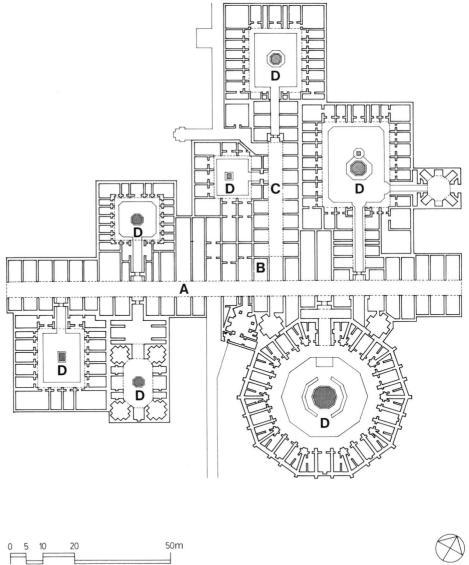

Plan 17 Part of the bazaar at Kashan, illustrating the complexity of Islamic planning. Its spine is a straight street (A) with shops (B) opening off it. Occasionally, however, these openings lead to corridors (C) from which in turn a series of variously shaped courtyards are entered (D), each with its fountain.

0 5 10 20 50m

**Bagh-i Delgosha
Shiraz**

This 18th-century garden is in north-east Shiraz near the Mausoleum of Sadi. Its name means 'Garden of the Heart's Delight'. At one time there had been a long canal, a pool and fountains, flower beds and orange trees, as well as a Qajar home. Presently, the garden is overrun and dry, but it is in the process of being restored. Mountains form a barren backdrop to the north.

**Bagh-i Eram
Shiraz**

The large 19th-century 'Garden of Paradise' is located in west Shiraz, with a mountain range to the north. Containing orange and lemon groves, its main walk is bordered by cypress trees. A Qajar pavilion contains a tiled summer room at a lower level, through which a water channel runs. A large reflecting tank in front of the pavilion supplies a narrow channel. There are many flowers, including a garden of roses. Well maintained, the Bagh-i Eram is typical of Iranian architecture and garden art of the last century.

**Bagh-i Gulistan
(Afifabad)
Shiraz**

Termed a 'rose garden', this extensive garden is located west of the city. Set out in the mid-19th century, it has a pavilion of local stone with many rooms and a large internal reception hall. Large pools with fountains are adjacent. Formerly owned by the Shah, it has been well maintained. There are extensive areas of grass, many stately trees and numerous rose bushes.

Plan 18, 19   Two gardens of Shiraz, the Bagh-i Eram (*left*) and Bagh-i Gulistan (*right*). In both, entrance is from the north (A) and a central pavilion (B) looks out over reflecting pools (C).

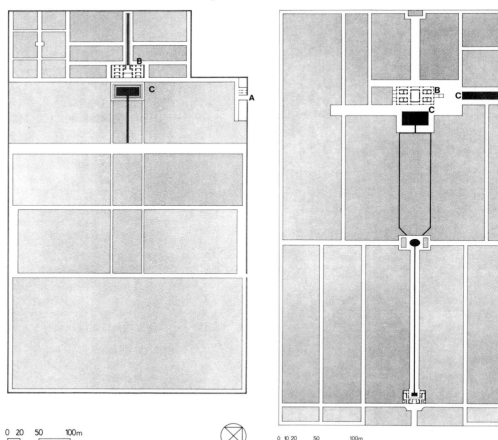

146 A barren mountain-side looms over a line of trees bounding the Bagh-i Delgosha in Shiraz. Once well maintained, this garden is now overgrown, but restoration has been attempted.

147 (*far right*) Looking down the straight central canal of the Bagh-i Eram in Shiraz. A garden of relatively late date, its water, trees, shrubs and many flowers provide a refreshing contrast to the dry mountain range beyond the trees in the background.

148 A view of the central pavilion of the Bagh-i Gulistan at Shiraz, seen here reflected in the long tank that leads from the entrance. The pavilion is large, and the garden is over 500 metres long.

**Bagh-i Khalili
Shiraz**

This late garden, hidden behind blank walls in a residential street near the river, west of the city, has a garden pavilion and luxuriant vegetation of great variety. Among its flowers are Bougainvillaea, roses, geraniums and water lilies. There are also several pools, one of them exceptionally curvilinear in shape.

**Narenjestan-i
Qavam
Shiraz**

The name of this small garden refers to its orange trees. A central canal links a series of pools lined with blue enamelled tiles to a straight-sided tank in front of an elegant 19th-century house. As customary, the principal rooms face south and are above the level of the pool and garden. The garden is flanked by palm trees, with high walls on the boundary. A set of rooms behind an arcaded wall cuts out the activities of the busy street to the south, while a right-angled turn in the entry lobby to the garden affords visual privacy.

**Haft Tan and
Chehel Tan
Shiraz**

Meaning 'Seven Bodies' and 'Forty Bodies', respectively, the names refer to the graves both these gardens contain. Possibly late 18th century, these gardens are hidden behind the customary high walls. At the end is a pavilion across the full width, with a pool in front. The main rooms of the pavilion are above the level of the garden and face south. There are orange trees and tall pines.

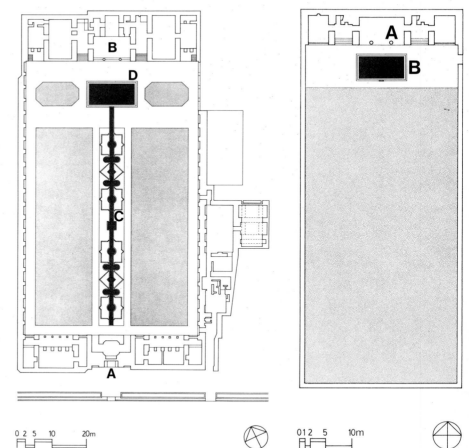

Plan 20   Narenjestan-i Qavam, Shiraz (*right*). Entrance (A) and house (B) face each other down one of the most elaborate of all Islamic garden canals (C), with a rectangular pool (D) at the far end.

Plan 21   Haft Tan, Shiraz (*far right*): the usual pavilion (A) overlooking a pool (B), and then a long expanse of garden, here containing graves.

130

149 An unusually sinuous pool in the Bagh–i Khalili, Shiraz. There is a great variety of flowers including roses, geraniums and water lilies as well as a good number of shade trees in this attractive garden.

150 A view from the window of the house that faces the Narenjestan–i Qavam in Shiraz. Next to the house is a terrace that contains a rectilinear tank. From this tank, down the centre of the garden, flows a narrow channel, punctuated by square, circular and oval pools lined with rich blue tiles.

151 A view of the graves in the Haft Tan, Shiraz, from which the garden derives its name (literally, 'Seven Bodies'). Apart from the tombstones, the design of this garden, with its south-facing pavilion, terrace, pool and walled enclosure, is of almost classic simplicity.

**Tombs of Sadi and
Hafez
Shiraz**

Sadi was a 13th-century poet, philosopher and narrator. Among his major works were *The Rose Garden (Gulistan)* and *The Orchard (Bustan)*. Hafez was a master of lyric poetry in the 14th century. Their mausolea, which resemble pavilions, are recent, as are the accompanying gardens, but they receive many visitors, continue the Iranian garden tradition and are well maintained.

152 Shallow pool in the garden of the Tomb of Hafez at Shiraz. The details of the garden, dedicated to Iran's famous 14th-century poet, are modern, but the dark pool filled to the brim and containing fountains belongs to a tradition established centuries earlier.

**Shah Goli
Tabriz**

The city of Tabriz in the north-west receives more precipitation than the plateau, and water supply is adequate. The Royal Pond (Shah Goli) is located east of the city and dates from the 18th-century Qajar period. Its main feature is a large artificial lake, square in shape, fed by hillside springs. An octagonal two-storey pavilion is located near the centre of the lake and is linked to one side by a causeway. The adjacent hill contains fruit trees on its terraces, and from its crest the view is panoramic. The water level of the lake is near the rim of its retaining wall, and as a result it seems to be poised over the surrounding valley.

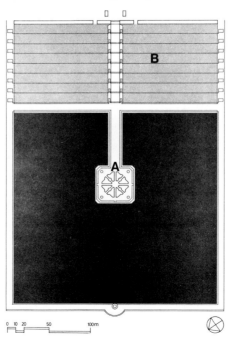

Plan 22 Shah Goli, Tabriz: an unusual garden consisting of a pavilion (A) in the middle of an artificial lake, connected by a causeway to a series of terraces (B) planted with fir trees.

132

153　The octagonal pavilion – perhaps once crowned by a dome – set in the large artificial lake, or Royal Pond, at Tabriz. Viewed from the adjacent hill, the water seems to hover over the surrounding valley.

Fathabad Tabriz

This private garden is near Shah Goli, east of Tabriz. A large orchard surrounds the garden, down the centre of which runs a channel. The ground has been gently terraced, and there are small waterfalls at the breaks of level, as well as gushing fountains in the centre of variously shaped small pools along the length of the channel. The channel and side paths are bordered with flowers, and there are many plants in pots. The channel ends at a deep stone-lined pool in front of a house which has replaced an earlier pavilion. The garden is shaded by great trees, an easier accomplishment in this region, with its higher annual rainfall.

Nearby at Shahvanak, Shalvar Jig, and surrounded by fields, there are the remains of a much older garden with a stone-edged channel and rectangular pool, now in disuse and overgrown.

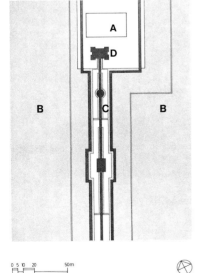

0 5 10　20　　50m

Plan 23　Fathabad, Tabriz: the house (A) and garden are set between two large areas of orchard (B). There are the usual axial channel (C) and pool (D).

133

Facing page
154 A view towards the southern, upper end of the garden at Fathabad near Tabriz. The circular pool is near the end of the canal, close to the house (see plan). Beyond it the path rises by a series of steps.

155 The large, stone-lined pool with centrally placed fountain-head, at the lower level of the garden in front of the house.

156 A courtyard in the Nematollah Valli Shrine at Mahan, near Kerman. This court is one of three, and has an octagonal pool shaded by cypresses and pines; the domed and tiled building that houses the tomb lies beyond. The precincts are cool, shady and quiet; the still water responds to stray breezes, while outside lies the lavender-coloured backdrop of mountains.

Nematollah Valli Shrine Mahan

Located in a large village twenty-three miles from Kerman, the shrine houses the tomb of Sayyid Shah Nematollah, a 15th-century poet and mystic. The first building was erected by a Muslim king of India, and the shrine received later additions from the Safavids and Qajars. Three courts, with pool and trees, are laid out between buildings on a central axis. In one of the inner courts is a cross-shaped pool, with an octagonal pool at its centre. There are tall cypress and pine trees, and many roses in pots. In the midst of a dry plain, with the mauve Kuh-i Jupar as backdrop, two slender blue and white minarets and central dome locate the shrine. Within its walls, the garden is cool and shaded, while the dark glimmering pools tranquilly reflect the brick and tile-faced buildings that surround them.

Gulistan Palace Teheran

Built at the turn of the 18th century by the Qajar, Fath Ali Shah, the building's deep and shady porch overlooking the garden is well suited to the climate. Outside there are blue faience pools, courts, some of which are paved in marble, and tall trees, mostly cypress and pine. The principal open garden contains large grassed areas in which anemones, daffodils, carnations and tulips are planted.

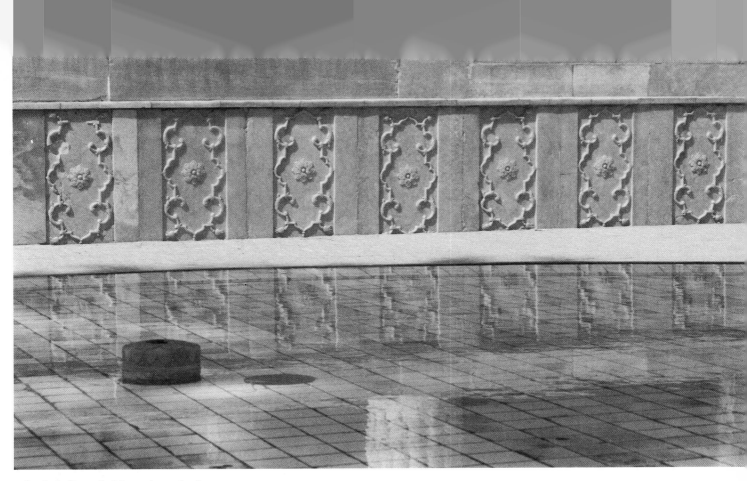

158 A shallow, tiled fountain pool reflects
the carved facing to the platform of a porch
at the Gulistan Palace in Teheran. The
depth of this porch always ensures some
shade in summer, while if necessary an
awning can be added to project still further
over the pool.

< 157 A general view of the Gulistan Palace
garden, with a tiled pool filled to the brim in
the foreground. Both traditional and more
recent features are to be found in this Qajar
garden, but the ancient objective of
providing shade and quietude in the midst of
a bustling city is beautifully achieved.

Mughal India

Setting IT IS ON THE PLAINS OF INDIA and in Kashmir that most of the Mughal gardens are situated. Delhi and Agra (110 miles to the south) are both beside the Jumna River; Lahore is located on the Ravi. The climate of the area is tropical, and winds are warm and dry. The heat increases from March to June, but its intensity is broken by the monsoon rains during July and August. It is the monsoon that supplies water for agriculture, although sometimes it causes severe flooding of the rivers, which from time to time change their courses. The natural landscape of this part of the subcontinent is flat, moderately fertile and only relieved by a winding river and occasional trees.

In great contrast is the Vale of Kashmir. Situated within the Himalayas some 400 miles north of Delhi, its summers are warm, and it lies protected from the monsoons by the surrounding mountains; winters can be cold. The ground is very fertile, and produces many crops. Rice fields are contoured to the sides of the hills, and chenar, poplar and willow trees abound. The Emperor Jahangir wrote:

> Kashmir is a garden of eternal spring or an iron fort to a palace of kings – a delightful flower-bed, and a heart-expanding heritage for dervishes. Its pleasant meads and enchanting cascades are beyond all description. There are running streams and fountains beyond count. Wherever the eye reaches there are verdure and running water.

The subcontinent has a long-standing tradition of gardens, and accounts of some form of irrigation, as well as parks, date back over an extensive period. Two thousand years ago, King Ashoka ordered the development of gardens and parks with pools and shaded walks. He prized plants for their fragrance and fruit, and, as apparently was customary, planted them informally. Wall-paintings, rock-carvings and Sanskrit literature several hundred years later depicted gardens with tanks, channels, fountains and lily ponds; and subsequent development of the use of tanks and pools has been confirmed in many records. Gardens were attached to Buddhist seminaries and monasteries, where they were open to public access, and later to the houses of princes, nobles and merchants, although here they were screened for privacy and to avoid envy. Merchants were accustomed to introduce plants as gifts, and, with the growth of trade and cultural contacts between India and Central Asia, there is little doubt that Indian tradition even influenced early Iranian gardens.

The picture becomes more comprehensive from the time of Firoz Shah, an early Muslim Sultan who ruled six hundred years ago. This most enterprising ruler is reputed to have established 200 towns, 50 dams and 30 reservoirs, as well as many scores of gardens in and around Delhi. Although these gardens were mainly orchards, they had irrigation channels and many fountains. The ordered, geometrical planning Firoz Shah encouraged was in contrast to the free layout of the Buddhist gardens it replaced, although the quadrapartite plan was already to be found in the Hindu temple gardens of south India, as well as in the crossing of the two main streets of the traditional Indian village. The

159 The central canal of the Taj Mahal, leading from the mausoleum itself to the red sandstone gate-house seen here. The vista is reinforced by the row of carved sandstone fountains, which are placed only on the north–south axis. This view is in the opposite direction to that seen in plate 5.

design of the Mughal garden as it is now known was further anticipated when, two hundred years after Firoz Shah, a square garden attributed to one Baz-Bahadur was established with a pool as well as a pleasure house in the centre. There were trees and flowers, and his palace contained fountains and tanks with coloured tiles.

There were many royal gardens in the south. Water, and particularly running water, was popular. There were fountains and cascades, and traces still remain of channels, cisterns and wells. There was even a garden city near 15th-century Baroda, the Islamic capital of Gujarat.

It was under the Mughals, however, that the Islamic garden tradition reached its height. The Mughals were descended from the Mongols in Central Asia. Babur, the first Mughal Emperor, was directly descended from Genghis Khan and Tamerlane, each of whom had conquered parts of the Iranian Empire. The Mongols spread the Islamic religion and culture over vast territories, and Tamerlane took architects, artists, poets and garden designers to enrich his capital at Samarkand. Gardens established in this city boasted pavilions, avenues lined with trees, and fountains; many of the gardens bore Iranian names. These were the gardens that impressed the young Babur. Having twice conquered but finally lost Samarkand, Babur subsequently turned to India. He invaded the subcontinent from his base in Kabul, and in the early 16th century proclaimed himself ruler in Delhi. While the shrewd Babur was mainly concerned with achieving his own ambitions, he also appreciated the beauty of gardens and laid out several in India. The first of these was possibly the Ram Bagh at Agra, and this was followed by others both on the plains and in Kashmir.

During the time of the Mughal Emperors there were many contacts between their own and the Iranian courts. Marriages were arranged, officials were exchanged and Persian, the source of present-day Urdu, was the court language. All the Mughal Emperors from Babur to Aurangzeb were familiar with the Iranian garden of paradise. They loved gardens, established them, spent time in them, were fully knowledgeable about their design, planting and maintenance and recorded their accomplishments in these areas.

The evolution of the Mughal garden reflects a cycle found in many creative periods of art. Beginning with Babur's Ram Bagh, the development reached its most creative phase under Jahangir, was taken to perfection under Shah Jahan and declined under Aurangzeb. This cycle also paralleled development in the empire as a whole, and reflected the availability of revenue for gardens and related works.

Concept On arriving in Agra, Babur recounted how he established his first garden.

> One of the great defects of Hindustan being its lack of running-waters, it kept coming to my mind that waters should be made to flow by means of wheels erected wherever I might settle down, also that grounds should be laid out in an orderly and symmetrical way. With this object in view, we crossed the Jun-water to look at garden-grounds a few days after entering Agra. Those grounds were so bad and unattractive that we traversed them with a hundred disgusts and repulsions. So ugly and displeasing were they, that the idea of making a Char-bagh in them passed from my mind, but needs must! as there was no other land near Agra, that same ground was taken in hand a few days later.

Eventually he began by sinking a well and forming a tank, and he followed this by building apartments and indoor baths. 'Three things oppressed us in

Hindustan,' Babur went on to say, 'its heat, its violent winds, its dust. Against all three the Bath is a protection, for in it, what is known of dust and wind? and in the heats it is so chilly that one is almost cold.' The layout of the garden in regular formation followed, and roses and narcissus were planted. Babur probably designed the garden himself. Stonecutters, carpenters and diggers were mentioned and were possibly imported, but no architect was named. Certainly the Emperor was interested and knowledgeable enough to accomplish the work himself.

Babur was interested in the garden as an object of beauty and a means of delight, rather than as a man-made reflection of the Quranic image of paradise. He soon found that the hot dry plains of 'that charmless and disorderly Hind' were unsuitable for the orchards and vineyards to which he was accustomed in Kabul and Samarkand. As a result, there commenced a development of the open layout and greater architectural character eventually to be so typical of the Indian garden.

The Islamic garden tradition of order, geometry, symmetry, straight channels and rectilinear pools also absorbed local custom. Hindu craftsmen introduced an organic quality. Carved columns, lintels and eaves and carvings of flowers were all accepted in Mughal garden pavilions and courtyards, and the irregular planning of Fatehpur Sikri provides further illustration of their influence. There were precedents for Babur's garden plans; however, he now provided a new direction and impetus. From now on, garden designer and water engineer collaborated with Emperor or architect at the outset, and a unified composition was the result. Stone tanks, stone-lined water channels and water chutes completely integrated the Mughal palace, mausoleum or kiosk with its garden.

Following Islamic principles of order, Mughal garden layouts were geometrical, with deliberate divisions and subdivisions. The prototype plan was flat, almost two dimensional, and was as easily adapted to the plain of the Ganges as it had been to the Iranian plateau. Yet level terrain not only encouraged retention of the traditional *char bagh* pattern, but invited greater magnificence and size as well. Sites were chosen with imagination, and terraces overlooked the river from the Taj Mahal as well as from the forts of Delhi and Agra.

It was Kashmir, with its attractive natural sites and abundant water, that was to provide a new stage in the evolution of the Islamic garden, even though the traditions and strengths of the original concept were retained. Extended use was made of the garden by introducing the secluded *zenana*, or women's terrace; corner pavilions were introduced, which overlooked the surrounding fertile countryside, so linking the paradise garden with the outside world. Furthermore, although surrounding walls were retained, they were modified so that the adjacent hills and trees could be seen, and in this way there was a greater merging of the garden with the outer landscape; within and without there was ample contrast. On the one hand, there was the geometry and symmetry of the layout, and on the other the organic form of the planting, the brilliant colour of the flowers, and the constant movement and sparkle of water (the hilly landscape encouraged the introduction of waterfalls). All of these, together with the stone, marble and inlay of the palaces, tombs and pavilions within the gardens, served as a high relief to the surrounding hills, countryside and towns.

The gardens designed by Babur were often constructed in a series of ascending terraces, and this concept was followed in many later gardens. Some of the royal gardens, such as Shalamar at Lahore, or Shalamar and Achabal in Kashmir, had three terraces: the first level was open to the public, when the Emperor sat in audience; the second was his private garden; and the third was the *zenana* garden for the harem. A Mughal garden could have eight terraces, which followed the Islamic concept of paradise in eight divisions. Alternatively, a garden could have seven divisions, which then reflected the seven planets. There was little consistency; Nishat Bagh in Kashmir was given twelve divisions, one for each sign of the Zodiac.

Terraced Mughal gardens were usually approached from the lowest level, which gave a sense of anticipation when regarding the upper terraces. The focus of design for the pleasure garden was a pavilion, and when located at a lower level, it afforded a view of the garden ahead, often with its mountain backdrop beyond. More often, however, the pavilion was located on the topmost terrace, and then not only the garden, but the surrounding countryside could be seen. On flat ground, where sweeping views were impossible, the central structure was raised on a platform, to impart a degree of grandeur and to make the most of the view. On these occasions, the pavilion or mausoleum was at the centre of the traditional *char bagh*.

There were other typical elements of the Mughal garden which had a strong architectural character: channels were sometimes laid at right-angles to the main water course, and conformed to the traditional four-fold division. These channels were paralleled by straight paths, while the area between was grassed, edged with narrow flower beds and shaded by straight rows of imposing trees. The garden was enclosed by massive walls, with serrated battlements and corner turrets at the inner angles, which gave protection from brigands as well as a sense of privacy and peace. The walls were a shield against the hot winds of summer and the blown sand. Lofty gateways, centred in the wall, contained huge wooden doors, studded with heavy iron bosses, nails and pikes. Regular avenues led from the gateway or flanking pavilion to a central structure in front of which were rectangular water tanks. Water flowed through carved inclined planes or chutes (*chadar*) from one terrace level to the next.

Mughal gardens were divided predominantly between those surrounding a mausoleum, and those developed for pleasure. The Mughal mausoleum set in its garden was not derived from Iranian precedents; it is more likely to have evolved from Mongol tradition or even from Hindu mythology. A garden would be developed during the owner's lifetime, when the building at its centre was possibly used for receptions and banquets, and then converted into a mausoleum at his death. The Tomb of Itimad-ud-Daula for example, was a garden house before its function was changed. Once a garden contained a mausoleum, it was open to the public. The plan of the mausoleum garden was simply based on the *char bagh*. Channels and pools radiated from the various façades, and associated water devices formed an integral and dignified part of the tomb setting. An exception to the customary centred layout was the Taj Mahal, where the building was placed at the end of its garden. Here, poised against the sky, the mausoleum overlooked the Jumna.

Gardens in the plains were more related to the traditional formal paradise layout, and were primarily the setting for magnificent buildings. The development of the pleasure garden, on the other hand, largely reflected the regard felt by the Mughal Emperors for Kashmir, where many such gardens were established. Great royal processions moved northward from the hot dusty plains to spend the summer in the Vale. It was in Kashmir, with its green hills, mountain streams and fertile fields, that paradise seemed truly on earth.

Gardens here were set mainly on the lower slopes of the surrounding mountains. In these locations there was an abundance of water. There was also a magnificent view of the surrounding countryside. Not only were these gardens used to entertain friends and family of the court and nobility, but they provided a worthy setting for court ceremonial. Shelter and comfort were provided by trees, many of which bore fruit; awnings of canvas and waxcloth shaded carpets, brocades, velvets and embroidered silk furnishings. Developed primarily for enjoyment, the pleasure gardens were also regarded as an opportunity for aggrandizement and display. Yet there were refinements. Some gardens were dedicated to a single flower, and some, perhaps reflecting Hindu influence, were intended to be seen only by moonlight.

Courtyards were also largely for pleasure, when they were designed as small enclosed gardens with water, grass and shade. The majority of such courts are located in the forts of Lahore, Agra and Delhi, and, together with many buildings in the plains, they exhibited refined design, good use of materials and skilled workmanship. When courtyards were attached to mosques they had a very different and more serious purpose; they were still well designed and executed, were predominantly paved and contained an ablution basin in the centre.

Water   Irrigation in India, even before the Mughals, depended on artificial lakes, canals and wells, with water raised by an arrangement of wheels and levers. Systems of water supply were developed and extended by Babur and his successors. A well was the source of water for Babur's first garden at Agra, as well as for the complex of gardens and courts at Fatehpur Sikri and Akbar's Tomb at Sikandra. From the well, it was fed into storage tanks and thence to a pond and channels. Alternatively, as at the Taj Mahal, water was drawn from the river by a system of buckets before it was stored in a reservoir.

In Kashmir, which provided the most attractive sites, water was easier to obtain. In fact, the general abundance of water in Kashmir provided a challenge to exploit it. Sometimes the open channel which flowed through the gardens was fed directly from a small river or stream, as at Shalamar or Nishat Bagh, or sited at the source of a spring, as at Verinag or Achabal. These gardens, with spring or stream as immediate source, managed more easily to retain their original freshness and vitality. Fortunately, the potential of water was thoroughly understood. Tanks, canals, waterfalls, chutes and fountains were employed in profusion, their design carried out with skill and imagination. Not surprisingly, the nature of water, its taste and coolness often formed the subject of discussion. At the Red Fort in Delhi, as well as at Fatehpur Sikri, the water that flowed through the chamber for the use of the Emperor and his family was heated. Generally, however, the water's natural coolness encouraged the situating of pavilions surrounded by tanks and the spray of fountains, as well as the placing of stone thrones or slabs across channels at the edge of waterfalls.

Tanks were constructed from which the water was distributed. These tanks or basins were carved with flowing patterns, which in a way seemed to compensate for the static nature of the water within them. But except in the courtyard of a mosque, the still surface of a pool had less appeal than water in movement. The spray of fountains, the splash of a jet, the foam at the foot of a *chadar*, the ripple and glitter of a swift-flowing channel and the full range of their sounds all provided great pleasure. Only limitations of pressure and supply restrained the use of fountain-heads and further lavish display. Both ornament and utility were served when a fine jet fell into an elaborately carved basin set in the stone floor of a pavilion, or when a series of fountains set down the centre of a canal moistened and cooled the air around them.

The channels of the earlier Mughal gardens, as at the Tomb of Humayun, were narrow and shallow, with broad areas of paving on each side. Secondary channels led from the main ones. As Mughal garden design evolved, the channels became wider, and the expanse of water in the centre of Shalamar Bagh, Lahore, reflects a full design assurance. But so strong was the influence of water in both early and late Mughal gardens, that today its presence is felt even if, owing to restricted water supply, it is in fact absent.

The base of channels was sometimes inlaid with zig-zag stripes of dark marble to symbolize the movement of waves as the water flowed through. Sometimes these stripes had small ridges to disturb the water in its passage; but more often such carving was reserved for the water chutes, which were given a multiplicity of linear and scalloped patterns. This richness of expression is found even in gardens on the plain, when the water had to be raised from a well, and changes in level were slight. In Kashmir, the height of falls was greater, and various carved chutes broke the water into curves ripples, pearl drops or striated sheets. Bubbling as it flowed from one level to the next, the water recalled the white foam of the clear mountain stream as it sped over the rocks, and graphically illustrated why the chute was termed a *chadar*, or white shawl.

A series of carved recesses or niches (*chini-kana*) behind a waterfall was also often found in the Mughal garden. By day they held small vases of flowers; by night, as the moving film of water glossed in front of them, candles glittered. Three hundred years ago, describing the water at Achabal, the traveller and physician Bernier wrote: 'its fall maketh a great Nape of thirty or forty paces long, which hath an admirable effect, especially in the night, when under this Nape there is put a great number of little Lamps fitted in holes purposely made in the Wall; which maketh a curious shew'. Today's use of the word 'curious' has evolved. There is no doubt that the stone-carved *chini-kana* at Achabal, others in Kashmir and the carved marble recesses at Shalamar Bagh, Lahore, and the Red Fort at Delhi must have afforded a magnificent spectacle.

Planting Many varieties of trees were planted in the Mughal garden, and their range was extended by imports from other regions, such as the poplar from Italy and the oriental plane or chenar from Asia Minor. Typical of trees in Kashmir gardens were the poplar, dark cypress, willow and particularly the massive chenar. The scale of the chenar linked garden to lake in front and mountain at rear, strikingly realized at Nishat Bagh. Chenars also provided a distinctive form and much shade. At Naseem Bagh they formed the whole garden, while they also gave significance to the tiny island in the midst of Dal Lake that bears their name. These trees were planted in rows, shading a canal and its adjacent paths, or were planted in clusters amidst the grass.

Adequate information is available on the planting of a Mughal garden. The *Institutes of Akbar* (*Ain-i-Akbari*), besides listing the customs and regulations of the Mughal Empire, includes the names of garden plants, such as roses, violets, sunflowers and jasmine. Peter Mundy, a traveller in the 17th century, ascribed to the gardens of Agra apples, oranges, figs, mangoes, coconuts, bananas and mulberries, as well as roses, marigolds, poppies and carnations, which were all watered by hand during the extensive dry season. Other fruits in the Mughal garden were lime, quince, apricot, cherry, plum, peach, guava, pear, pomegranate and tamarind. Flowers also were valued by both Hindu and Buddhist, and were appreciated as much in India as in Iran. Hollyhocks, wallflowers, delphiniums, hibiscus, hyacinths, jasmine, lilies, narcissus, lotus, lilacs and tulips could be added as well. Iris took the place of myrtle; frequently present in Mughal iconography, it grew away from the heat in the shade of tombs, and was hence known as 'the graveyard bulb'.

But the garden was more to the Mughals than a place of flowers. It demonstrated a profound sense of site and a strong composition, which reflected the Muslim concern for order and delight in geometry. A practical knowledge of trees and plants was combined with a thorough understanding of water. A miniature of the Feast of the Birth of Humayun, painted at the end of the 16th century, depicts some of the basic design elements: the square tank with fountains, the central watercourse, a stone platform on which the Emperor was seated, shaded by a canopy, flowers, a chenar and cypress trees. This is a very attractive rendering, and illustrates how fully gardens entered into the lives of the Mughal Emperors. Gardens were established at intervals on the route between the Deccan and Kashmir, and the Emperors themselves saw to their design. It was in gardens that they often held their court. They pitched their tents on the grass beneath the trees and, from stone platforms beside the cascades, overlooked the beauty that they had helped to create.

The Fort Agra

This fort was built by Akbar in the second half of the 16th century, and took eight years to complete. Its red sandstone walls stand as they were originally, but many of the very early sandstone buildings within were replaced by marble palace structures by Shah Jahan. The various levels offer open and enclosed views as well as unexpected vistas; the final view attained is that over the Jumna River with the Taj Mahal in the distance.

The 'Fish Square' (Machahi Bhawan) was a royal garden, with tanks that contained fish, until ransacked by the Jats in the 18th century. It once contained flower beds, fountains and channels; now, apart from the open terrace overlooking the Jumna River, its two-storey arcade merely encloses a grassed space.

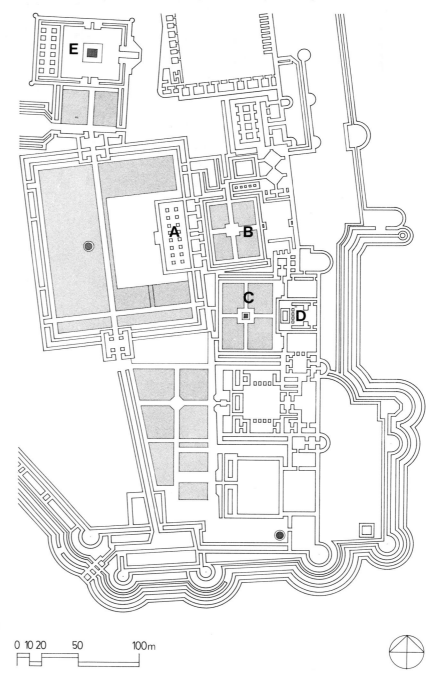

Plan 24 The fort at Agra is a miniature town, with palaces and courtyards and mosques. The most notable are A, the Diwan-i-Am; B, the Machahi Bhawan ('Fish Square'); C, the Anguri Bagh (see plan 25); D, the Khas Mahal; and E, the Moti Masjid (see plan 26).

0 10 20   50   100m

160 In the centre of the Anguri Bagh is a raised tank with steps leading to it on the east and west sides. Behind to the left is seen the Khas Mahal, in front of which is a cascade.

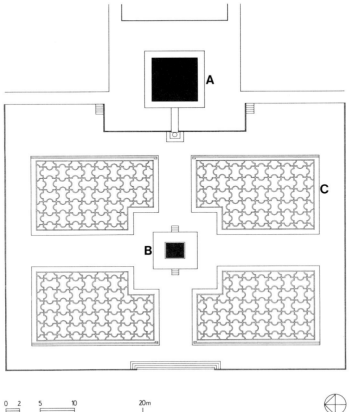

Plan 25 The Anguri Bagh ('Grape Garden') consists of a square pool (A) connecting the Khas Mahal with the garden; in the centre is a raised tank (B) surrounded by the four quarters of the *char bagh* (C).

0 2 5 10 20m

161 Inside the fort at Agra: water flowing down an inlaid and carved chute reached a small carved pool, from which it overflowed into shallow runnels. The zig-zag motif of the *chadar* symbolizes the flow of water.

The 'Grape Garden' (Anguri Bagh) was used by the harem, and provides a good example of a garden located in the royal quarters. On three sides are apartments built by Akbar for the women attendants of the household. On the terrace in front of the Khas Mahal (the central marble hall or private palace) is a white marble tank with a cusped and foiled border. A shallow channel leads water to a cascade over carved niches into a small pool. The garden, intimate in scale, is divided into four. Marble is used and elaborately carved, while the pattern of the flower beds is intricately outlined in sandstone. Originally there would have been a rich variety of flowers as well as low shrubs in this *char bagh*, but not large fruit trees, which would have broken the view.

There are diverse areas within the fort, each attractive in its own way: the Moti Masjid is a mosque built simply but impressively entirely of white marble, with a rectangular ablution basin in the centre of its courtyard; elsewhere, a myriad of convex mirrors glitters to candlelight on the walls of the antechambers to the royal bathrooms.

The Jumna was the main source of water, and the fort was served by a system of tanks, pipes and possibly by overhead aqueducts. The fort and its buildings have generally remained in good condition, in all likelihood protected by the various levels of ground, in contrast to the vulnerability of the flat site of the Delhi fort. Unfortunately, the pools, channels and fountains of the gardens and courtyards have for the most part long been dry. As at Delhi, the design stands in its own right without the water's presence, but it would certainly be the more attractive for it.

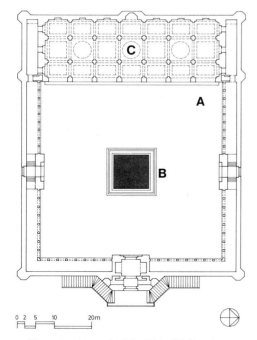

0 2 5 10 20m

Plan 26 Agra, the Moti Masjid (Pearl Mosque). On the edge of the fort complex, it contains the normal courtyard (A), ablution pool (B) and mosque proper (C).

162   The Pearl Mosque (Moti Masjid),
with its massive columns of hewn marble
and three well-proportioned domes, faces
the courtyard and ablution tank. Tank,
courtyard and mosque are all of white
marble.

163   A flight of steps leading to the Moti
Masjid, built on the highest ground in the
fort at Agra. Owing to the changes in level,
the buildings have a varied and dramatic
relationship to each other.

164 The north-west corner pavilion of the Ram Bagh with surmounting kiosk (*chhatri*) overlooking the Jumna River. When establishing his gardens after his arrival in Agra, Babur chose this location to afford protection against the heat, wind and dust.

165 (*below right*) Located some distance northward from the more frequently visited attractions of Agra, the Ram Bagh has fallen into disuse, and although preserved as a garden, its upkeep has been neglected.

Ram Bagh
Agra

The 'Garden of Rest' (Aram Bagh, or Ram Bagh) was one of several gardens established by Babur on the banks of the Jumna to recall those he had known in Samarkand and Kabul. Although long disused and lacking water, there is still a distinct order and geometry to the platforms and walks with their narrow water courses which were raised above the ground for ease of irrigation. Rooms and terraces overlook the Jumna River, and there were stone platforms on which the Emperor would sit, as well as paths, flowers, shrubs and fruit trees.

The garden was watered from a well at the highest point along its border with the Jumna. This led to a tank where the Emperor bathed in summer, and then into a pond; it continued through channels along the terrace and down chutes to further channels throughout the garden. The riverside pavilions were also supplied with water, and serving them underground was a complex system of cisterns and tanks.

This garden is the only one by Babur to survive in recognizable form. It is a little removed from Agra's more frequently visited gardens and has not been well maintained.

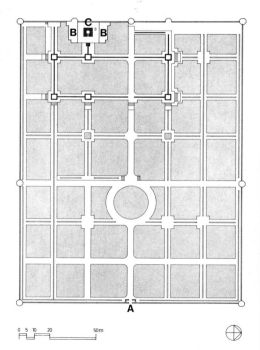

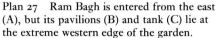

Plan 27 Ram Bagh is entered from the east (A), but its pavilions (B) and tank (C) lie at the extreme western edge of the garden.

**Taj Mahal
Agra**

Mumtaz Mahal was twenty-one when she became the second and favourite wife of the Emperor Shah Jahan. When she died in childbirth, a mausoleum was built to her memory. The Taj Mahal (Crown of the Palace) was constructed in the 17th century by 20,000 labourers, masons and stonecutters, using marble, sandstone and semi-precious stones brought, in some instances, from a very great distance.

Often described as floating, the building has a remarkable ethereal quality, changing with the light throughout the day. On one side of the white marble mausoleum is a red sandstone mosque, and this is balanced on the other side by a meeting house. Around the high entrance portico of the tomb are quotations from the Quran. Inside the building itself, the tomb replicas of Mumtaz and the Emperor are surrounded by intricately carved marble screens. The mausoleum's marble walls are inlaid with restrained pietra-dura in floral patterns; semi-precious stones are set within the dome and intermittently flash in the moonlight.

The building is located majestically at the end of the classic *char bagh* rather than at the centre, as would have been more usual. Similar to the Red Fort at Delhi, the large garden, walled on three sides, is open to the river on the fourth. The mausoleum is placed on a raised terrace, with four octagonal pavilions marking the corners; it is seen against the azure sky with the green of the garden, possibly designed by Ali Mardan Khan, in the foreground.

From the main entrance gateway, capped by twenty-two small kiosks or *chhatris*, steps lead down to a fountain-filled canal which in turn leads to the white marble mausoleum. Pathways bordering the canal are lined with slender dark green cypresses

166 The Taj Mahal, Agra, seen across a bend in the Jumna River from a terrace at the fort. This was the view that its builder, the Emperor Shah Jahan, saw every day after he had been imprisoned in the fort by his son Aurangzeb.

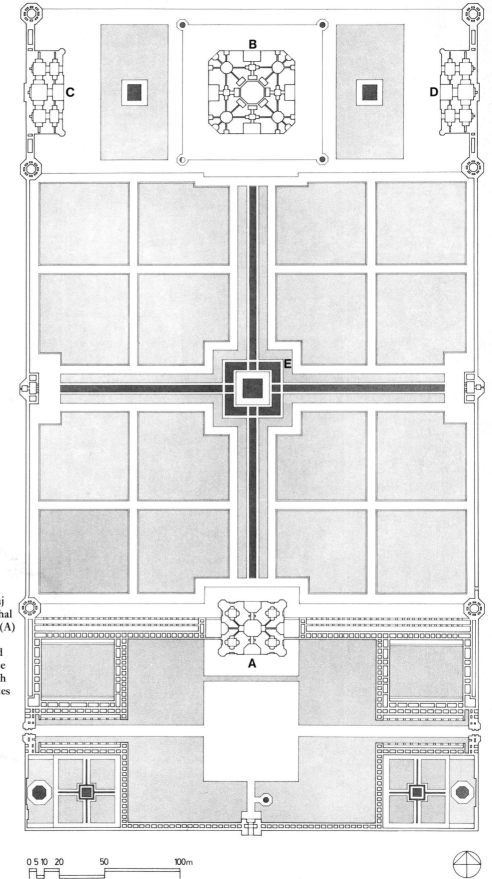

Plan 28   The grand simplicity of the Taj
Mahal Garden makes it a classic of Mughal
landscape design. The entrance pavilion (A)
is directly opposite the white marble
mausoleum (B) on its terrace. To left and
right are a mosque (C) and meeting house
(D). In the centre the raised tank (E) with
its channels in four main directions divides
the whole into the typical *char bagh*.

0 5 10 20   50   100m

167 The Taj Mahal gleams like an
unearthly vision, framed in the branches of
the large trees that surround the garden.

168 Corner detail of a pool on one of the
two terraces that flank the mausoleum. A
similar but more elaborate and finely carved
detail is found in the marble reflecting pool
at the centre of the garden.

which create a strong perspective towards the tomb, a perspective reinforced by the
row of fountains. An intended view of the Taj Mahal is from the raised marble tank
located at the cross-axes of the garden. The tank is symmetrical, with similar stairs and
benches on all four sides, and the mausoleum is reflected in the water.

The garden as a whole is divided into four by sandstone pathways, with a broad but
shallow water channel in the centre of each. These areas are further subdivided into
four smaller areas with grass, shrubs and tall trees. Stone and marble benches
encourage the enjoyment of various views. There are no *chadars* in this garden, only
fountains. These are laid solely on the main south–north canal, since fountains on the
east–west axis would have diverted attention from the mausoleum. An ingenious
system of copper pots at the base of each fountain stored the water until the pressure on
each was uniform, thus ensuring that the water from all fountains rose to the same
height.

Originally, water was drawn from the Jumna by a system of buckets, and collected in
reservoirs on the roofs of rooms in the middle of the walls bounding the garden. Today,
these reservoirs are fed by electric pumps working from a well. The garden is irrigated
by overflow from the canals. Specifically, underground pipes lead from the reservoirs
to the fountains and south–north canal, which connects to and feeds the east–west
canal. These canals are much wider than the narrow runnels found at the tombs of
Humayun and Akbar. The causeways are raised for irrigation, and the areas near the
canals which receive the most water are planted with flowers. Since larger trees are
found only in areas further away, this leaves unobscured the principal view of one of
the most beautiful buildings in the world.

169 A view of the terrace at the foot of the platform on which the Taj Mahal stands. The paving is composed of an interlocking pattern of red sandstone stars and white marble diamonds, seen in detail in plate 84. The low balustrades are of carved sandstone.

Tomb of Itimad-ud-Daula Agra

This site was originally the pleasure garden of the prime minister of the Emperor Jahangir, and its main pavilion was on the terrace overlooking the Jumna River. After his death in the early part of the 17th century, his daughter Nur Jahan, wife of the Emperor, built the mausoleum in the garden, as was customary.

The building is the first major example of fine inlay work in marble, a technique used later with great refinement in the Taj Mahal. All faces of the building are covered; the patterns are both geometric and naturalistic, and include cypresses, fruit trees and flowers.

The garden follows the *char bagh* pattern. In the centre stands the tomb; on each of the four sides of the plinth is a tank with a fountain in the middle. A *chadar* leads to shallow channels, now dry, that surround the centre platform; further channels run through slightly raised causeways to the four gateways at the centre of each wall, and around the garden's periphery. Water that overflowed the channels was used to irrigate the garden. Along the Jumna's bank two wells supplied the garden. Overhead tanks fed underground pipes to the fountains on the plinth.

Outside the enclosure between the main gate and the road is an orchard. This custom dates back to the days of the Timurids when an orchard separated by a high wall was usually attached to a pleasure garden, and the sale of the produce provided funds for the garden's upkeep after the owner's death.

Facing page below
170   The Tomb of Itimad-ud-Daula at the centre of its square garden at Agra. Channels surround the building, and from the centre of each side form links with a further channel on the periphery.

171   The shallow channel that edges its way round the garden opens out into small ponds by each of the gateways. Water was obtained from the Jumna River, and irrigated the garden by overflowing the channels, and pouring across and down the sides of the causeways.

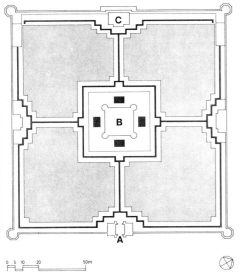

0 5 10 20   50m

Plan 29   The Tomb of Itimad-ud-Daula is the centrepiece of a formal garden with entrance (A), mausoleum (B) and pavilion (C) on a single axis.

Red Fort Delhi

The Red Fort at Delhi was built by Shah Jahan in the first half of the 17th century. Located on the bank of the Jumna River, it is entered from the city through a large gateway. At the end of the first court is the public audience hall (Diwan-i-Am), and between this hall and the river are the Emperor's private apartments as well as those of the *zenana*.

There were several gardens with a network of water channels. In fact, the Red Fort was originally planned as a great water palace. Water was drawn from the river to the Shah Bagh in the fort's north-east corner, from where it fell down a marble chute into a scalloped basin. It then fed the palace chambers along the east edge of the fort, and other buildings, courtyards and gardens through fountains, waterfalls, cascades and pools. The design of the various rooms and gardens was largely based upon this supply of water.

Water flowed through the whole length of the private apartments as well as their adjacent courtyards. It helped to cool them, and was visually attractive; the conversation of the court was doubtless accompanied by its murmur, although in the private audience hall (Diwan-i-Khas) in front of the Emperor's throne it flowed under the floor slab. In the *hammam*, heated water flowed through a series of rectangular marble pools. In the Rang Mahal is a large lotus basin carved out of marble; it had semi-precious stone inlay, and its centre is shaped as a floating lotus bud. Scented water once rippled over the whole surface, and the basin's carved facets seemed gently to move under it. Water throughout the fort was treated in a multiplicity of ways, and there was considerable delicacy of detail.

The 'Life-Giving Garden' (Hayat Baksh Bagh) is one and a half metres below the terrace on which stand the private apartments, and it received its water from it.

172 A view through the Emperor's apartments from the Khas Mahal through the private audience hall to the *hammam* (see plan 31). The apartments overlooked a garden to the west and the Jumna River to the east, while a shallow canal flowed through their entire length.

Originally, this garden was a square *char bagh*, and contained a broad central channel with fountains and cross bridges, flower beds and pathways, as well as a deep tank and two marble pavilions. Water fell over *chini-kanas*, niches, which during the day were full of flowers in gold and silver vases; at night there were wax candles, compared in an early account to 'stars and fleecy clouds . . . lighted under the veil of water'.

Since the days of the Mughal court, the fort has suffered through war and careless occupation. The 'Moonlight Garden' (Mahtab Bagh), planted with pale flowers such as lilies, narcissus and jasmine, has disappeared; and while the Hayat Baksh Bagh has retained its central pavilion and basin, it is now only one half its original size. A military garrison now occupies a large section of the garden, the gold overlay and silver-plated fountains have been stripped and water no longer flows through the Emperor's private apartments or along the garden channels. Yet, despite the absence of water, the gardens and pavilions that remain have been sympathetically restored and receive a constant number of visitors.

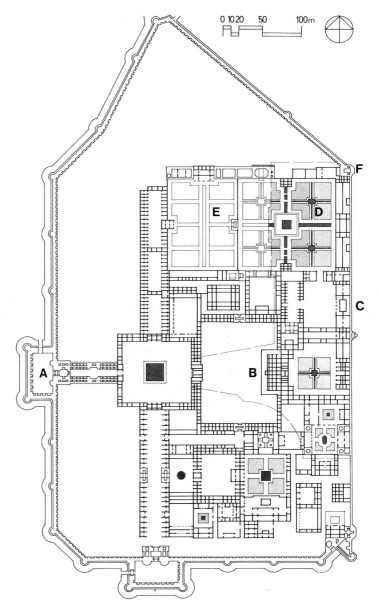

Plan 30 The Red Fort, Delhi, was entered through a ceremonial gate (A) which led through a large courtyard with central basin to the audience hall or Diwan-i-Am (B). The Emperor's private apartments (C) overlooked the Jumna River (see plan 31). Further north were the Hayat Baksh Bagh (D) and the Mahtab Bagh (E) – two gardens whose names mean 'Life-giving' and 'Moonlight' – and the Shah Bagh (F), a pavilion commanding the river bank.

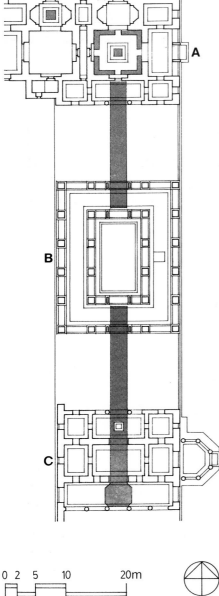

Plan 31   The Emperor's apartments in the
Red Fort, a sequence of bath, or *hammam*
(A), private audience hall, Diwan-i-Khas (B),
and private palace, Khas Mahal (C).

173   A marble pool in the *hammam* of the
fort's private apartments. Floors and dados
throughout the bath area are also of marble,
inlaid with floral patterns of multicoloured
stones. A hot or vapour bath was also
available.

174   The Hayat Baksh Bagh in the Red Fort: the platform in the foreground originally stood in the centre of a traditional *char bagh*. Trees provide shade, and the pavilion on the raised strip of land at the end of the garden overlooks the Jumna River.

175   Interior of the Shah Bagh in the north-east corner of the fort. The pavilion overlooks the Jumna River, from which water was drawn to fall down the chute into the basin at its foot. The water then continued by a shallow canal to the Emperor's apartments, from which it fed the gardens.

176 A carved basin of white marble in the courtyard of the Pearl Mosque. It has a simple inlay of floral design, and is surrounded by an overflow channel.

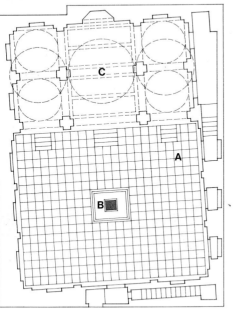

0 1 2   5   10m

Plan 32 The Pearl Mosque in the Red Fort, Delhi – the standard plan with courtyard (A) and ablution fountain (B) preceding the mosque itself (C).

177 The site of Humayun's Tomb at Delhi is flat, but minor changes of level were created artificially to produce the flow and ripple of water. Here water leaves a runnel to flow down a small carved sandstone *chadar* into a pool, before continuing its course. The octagon seen here combined the square, or material, aspect of man with the circle symbolizing eternity; symbolically, it also represented the divisions of the Quran.

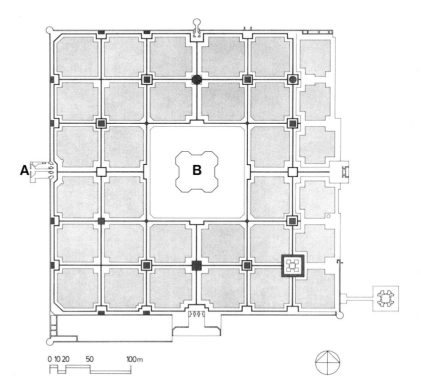

0 10 20   50   100m

Tomb of Humayun
Delhi

Humayun's Tomb was built by his widow, Hamida Begam, following the Emperor's death in the second half of the 16th century. It is a splendid example of the *char bagh* pattern. A walled garden is divided by broad causeways, and further subdivided into squares by smaller paths, with the occasional water basin at an intersection. Water was raised from a well on the periphery, and from there flowed through the garden's shallow runnels and tanks. The site is almost flat, but small *chadars* exploit a very slight gradient to the south.

This is the earliest Mughal garden that has been preserved in good condition, although there are now few trees, fewer flowers and no water. However, the scale of the garden is impressive, and it is a fitting site for the first substantial example of Mughal architecture.

178   The main axis of the Tomb of Humayun seen from the entrance. The mausoleum stands on a wide arcaded platform.

< Plan 33   The Tomb of Humayun. Entrance (A) is in the west. Traditionally, the mausoleum (B) stands in the middle of a symmetrical layout of canals and pools.

179   View from the terrace surrounding the Tomb of Humayun. Shallow pools are located at the intersections of the water channels. Marking the centre of each side of the wall surrounding the garden is a pavilion or gate-house, and one is seen here, terminating a vista.

**Achabal
Kashmir**

180 Fountains enliven a pool at Achabal in Kashmir. The reservoir near the mountain spring that feeds this garden also supplies the fountains with a strong head of water, and the sound of settling spray provides a delicate contrast to the rush of the continuously falling and swiftly flowing water in the adjacent channels.

This garden was possibly laid out by Nur Jahan, the wife of Jahangir, and is located about thirty miles south of Srinagar on the old Jammu route. It is watered by an ancient and once sacred spring from the adjacent hillside. The spring enters a reservoir above a great cascade, the climax of the garden, and builds up a head of water with sufficient pressure to serve the whole garden with its many fountains. Not only is the water of excellent quality, but it flows in sufficient abundance to feed the side channels that accompany the central course, while still leaving enough to supply the surrounding rice fields.

Achabal is a garden of light and shade. Its present pavilions are Kashmiri, and indigenous in character. They are pleasant enough, although not in keeping with the original Mughal spirit. From them, the surrounding water's variety of sound may be fully enjoyed. The channels glide and murmur, the fountains spray and splash, the chutes ripple and foam and the cascade tumbles, its bouncing droplets glittering in the strong sunlight that filters through the plane trees.

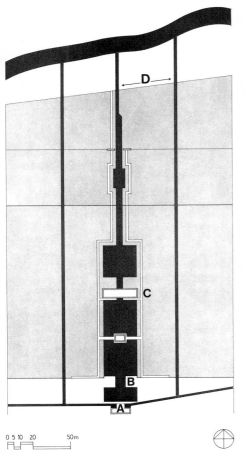

0 5 10 20   50m

181   There is a year-round abundance of water at Achabal.
Flowing rapidly over the *chadars*, its texture is broken before it
resumes its swift flow down the canals.

Plan 34   Achabal, Kashmir. The Kashmir gardens exemplify
linear design, with flowing water linking different levels. At
Achabal, water from the spring (A) descends by a cascade (B) to a
large rectangular pool with central platform. After going
underneath the pavilion (C) it eventually reaches the river, near a
modern road (D).

182   The view from Chashma Shahi on its hillside in Kashmir;
part of the garden is recent. Dal Lake may be seen beyond, and
another garden – Hari Parbat – rises in the distance.

**Chashma Shahi
Kashmir**

The 'Garden of the Royal Spring' was built by Ali Mardan Khan for Shah Jahan. Set into a mountainside overlooking Dal Lake, this small garden displays great changes in levels. Until relatively recently it enjoyed a spring which began in an upper pavilion and led from there down to the centre terrace, along a channel and through a pool simply containing a single jet. Flowing then through the principal pavilion, which contains an intimate view of the upper garden on one side and a panoramic view over Dal Lake on the other, the water fell down a further steep chute, along a channel and through a reservoir with five fountains and out. The completion of a government building in the vicinity has entailed the complete diversion of the water from this garden: a seemingly callous act. The present pavilions are Kashmiri, but rest on Mughal bases. The garden has been extended, providing further views of Dal Lake and its surroundings.

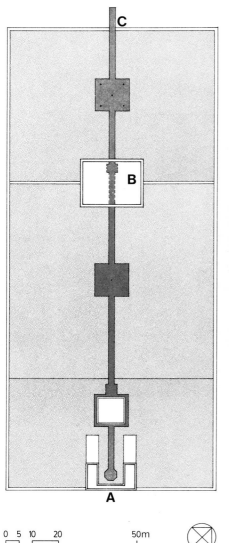

183   A small pool with a single jet. Apart from its hillside location, with its many flowers and trees, Chashma Shahi itself presents a very attractive spectacle. The recent diversion of its water has left channels dry, pools empty and fountains silent.

Plan 35   Chashma Shahi, Kashmir, has the familiar linear plan. Water from the spring (A) flows down through pools and channels through the pavilion (B) and out into Dal Lake. The entrance here (C) is at the lowest point.

0 5 10   20   50m

**Hari Parbat
Kashmir**

Constructed by Akbar at the end of the 16th century, Hari Parbat is reached by a short but steep climb after leaving the lake. The galleries around the summit afford full views of the surrounding countryside, which include Dal Lake and Srinagar. Water was hauled up in leather bags carried by mules. The fort was composed largely of soldiers' quarters, now in disrepair, and a small temple; there was also a garden on three levels, but this is now heavily overgrown.

The site is outstanding, and can be seen from many of the other gardens around the lake. On the summit, but surrounded by buildings, the garden is unusual and potentially dramatic: if it were restored, the journey by lake and on foot would be well worthwhile.

184 Akbar's fortress of Hari Parbat dominates the Kashmir city of Srinagar as well as the adjacent Dal Lake and Nagin Lake, from which this view is taken. From the summit one gains a panoramic view of the valley in all directions.

185 Although many parts of the fortress have fallen into ruin, it still contains many galleries, some of which are seen here. There is also a small temple and an overgrown water garden or tank, but there was no natural water supply.

165

**Naseem Bagh
Kashmir**

186   Naseem Bagh was the first of the Mughal gardens in Kashmir. All that remains now is the grid of chenars; once, no doubt, there were pavilions and terraces, but no trace of canals survives.

The 'Garden of Breezes' was the first Mughal garden in Kashmir, and was founded by Akbar. It faces east, and from its broad terraces there is a view over Dal Lake, with the mountains behind the gardens on the far side. Hundreds of chenars were laid out on a regular grid at Naseem Bagh by Shah Jahan; their stable mass reflected in the lake and contrasted with the shifting clouds above. The chenars could only be felled with royal permission. No architectural features of the garden remain, and there is no trace of water having been used. The grounds are now occupied by a regional engineering college.

**Nishat Bagh
Kashmir**

The 'Garden of Delight' is the largest on Dal Lake, and was laid out by Asaf Khan, the brother of Nur Jahan, wife of Jahangir. It is best approached by boat, when its series of terraces, originally twelve, are seen as a series of steps up from water level, with the mountains behind. The lower terraces provide a firm base to the composition. A central canal three metres wide links a series of cascades at the various changes of level. Jets play in pools as well as down the centre of each section of the canal; there is a slight design variation in each section, and in the carving of each *chadar*. At some points, a marble or stone platform (*chabutra*) overlooks the cascade, while the water flows beneath it to cool the air; each platform has a view across the garden to the lake. The canal is flanked by tall chenars, red and gold in the fall, and on each side of the garden is the traditional orchard. Along the full width of the *zenana* terrace is a high retaining wall, faced with a series of arches. At each end of this terrace, an octagonal corner pavilion of stone overlooks the poplars, the rice fields and the daily life of the world outside.

Today, a road cuts off the garden from the lake, reducing the number of its terraces; and the Kashmiri pavilion at the foot is obtrusive. But the water flows, the planting is tended and Nishat remains a monumentally splendid garden, seen and enjoyed by most visitors to Kashmir.

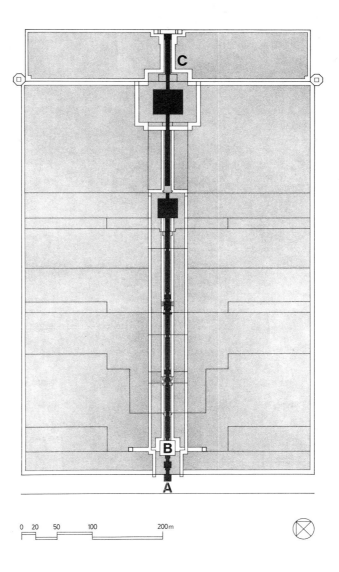

Plan 36 Nishat Bagh, Kashmir. The straight water channel is approached from the modern road (A) leading to a small pavilion (B). At the opposite end is the *zenana* terrace (C), where the women were secluded.

0 20 50 100 200m

187 Nishat Bagh, Kashmir, reflected in the waters of Dal Lake. The strong horizontal base formed by the lowest wall defines the edge of the garden, while its trees cluster behind. A modern road runs between the garden and the lake.

188 Water flowing over a *chadar* at Nishat Bagh. The pattern carved on each chute breaks the flow of water into foam, but in this case the movement is leisurely and still enables the carving beneath to be discerned.

**Pari Mahal
Kashmir**

'The Fairies' Palace' is one of the few legacies of Dara Shukoh, the ill-fated eldest son of Shah Jahan, who was usurped by his brother Aurangzeb. It is located on a hillside overlooking Dal Lake, and is laid out on a series of terraces. Since there are tanks, but no trace of waterfalls or canals, it may be assumed that the source of water was underground. Most of the architectural structure has fallen into disrepair; however, plants and grass are now tended, and the charm of its location, on a spur of rock with the mountains behind, remains.

189   The several levels of Pari Mahal are stepped up the hillside and supported by arcaded retaining walls. The garden structures are now in disuse, although some care is taken with planting.

Shalamar Bagh
Kashmir

190 Shalamar Bagh, Kashmir overlooks
Dal Lake and is connected to it by a long
canal. Here a clear reflection of poplars on
the surface of the lake is disturbed by the
gentle ripples from a passing *shikara*.

Facing page
191 The walls of Shalamar Bagh do not
confine it visually. Beyond them rise
majestic forest trees and beyond those again
– the garden's true boundary – the lake and
mountains of Kashmir.

170

The 'Abode of Love' was founded by Jahangir in honour of his wife, Nur Jahan. He
located it on an ancient site at the north-east end of Dal Lake, to which it is connected
by a long canal. The garden may easily be reached by road, but the finest approach is by
a quiet and slow skiff (*shikara*) across the lake, finally leading into an entry canal, to
which the garden forms a fitting climax. Indeed, one finds that, as with the other
gardens surrounding Dal Lake, lake and garden are in recollection inseparable.

The terraced garden is divided into three parts. The outer, or semi-public garden,
now truncated by a modern road, ends at the Diwan-i-Am. Water flows through this
pavilion, and, at the centre of the side where it falls into the tank below, stands a small
black marble throne. The second, or Emperor's garden, is slightly wider and contains
in its centre the Diwan-i-Khas. Much of the original building has been lost, but the
platform surrounded by fountains remains, as does the *hammam* on the north-west
boundary. The *zenana* is on the highest part of the site. It contains a central pavilion of
black marble, commissioned by Shah Jahan and carried out by Zafar Khan, the
Mughal governor of Kashmir. It stands surrounded by fountains and water, whose
glitter is reflected in the smooth polished marble.

A small river diverted from the rice fields just outside the far boundary wall supplies
the broad central canal that dominates the garden. The canal extends throughout the
length, its dark green water falling in smooth cascades over generally slight changes of
level. There are many fountain jets, and the canal is crossed by stepping-stones and
stone bridges. The raised stone border is softened by rose bushes. The central
pavilions provide a welcome area of shadow, from where the soothing flow of the
cascades may be heard. The air is moistened by the spray of the adjacent fountains.
Side canals are terminated by gateways in the enclosing wall.

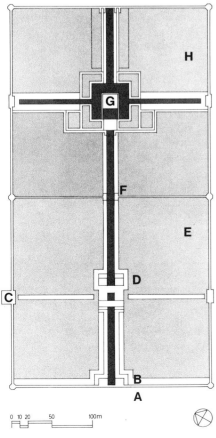

Tall chenars and poplar trees form a backdrop to the rose bushes and flowers bordering the canal, with further trees, fruit trees and flower parterres deliberately positioned. Behind all is the towering snow-capped Mahadev. There is an atmosphere at Shalamar Bagh of stately dignity and peace, even poetry, to which the water, flowers, trees and pavilions, well integrated, all contribute.

In the open, grassed areas, shaded here and there by tall trees, royal parties were once held. Courtiers reclined on carpets and watched dancing that was accompanied by a sitar, or listened to the recitation of poems by Sadi, Hafez and Khayyam. Today these areas are enjoyed by the public. On summer evenings, there is a sound and light show, but the majesty, simplicity and proportions of the garden itself remain a real tribute to the Mughals who created it three and a half centuries ago.

Plan 37   Shalamar Bagh is the most famous of the gardens round Dal Lake. The visitor enters at the lowest level from the modern road (A) occupying part of what was the public garden. The Diwan-i-Am (B) leads to the central canal, from which the *hammam* (C) and Diwan-i-Khas (D) are reached. All this area (E) is the Emperor's garden. Further up, along the canal with its small pavilions (F), one reaches the main pavilion (G), entirely surrounded by water; beyond this is the women's *zenana* (H).

192   Shalamar Bagh: light catches the
curved, vertical and horizontal surfaces of a
cascade and its foam as it pours into a basin
in the midst of the garden. Trees lend their
shade to cool the air already moistened by
the cascade and fountains.

**Verinag
Kashmir**

The location of this garden is about thirty-eight miles south of Srinagar. A favourite of
Jahangir and Nur Jahan, the design of this garden is the most simple of all. A deep clear
green octagonal pool is surrounded by an arcaded court. The pool contains a spring
which emerges from the hillside rising immediately behind. A long canal leads from the
pool and traverses the full length of the garden before it pours over a waterfall, leading
eventually into the Jhelum River. A magnificent natural setting contrasts with the
uniquely powerful, simple geometry of the garden itself.

193   Deodars clothe the hills which serve as
a backdrop at Verinag, Kashmir, to the
geometry of the canal. The octagonal pool at
the foot of the hill supplies water to irrigate
the garden.

194   Cool recesses behind arcades surround
the octagonal tank at Verinag. The deep,
green pool is fed from a spring within it, and
great trout may be seen just below the
surface. From this pool water flows under a
central arch into a long canal.

**The Fort
Lahore
Pakistan**

Lahore fort, located at the north-west angle of the city's former walls, was commenced by Akbar in the mid-16th century, and was extended by Jahangir, Shah Jahan and Aurangzeb. Together with the other great Mughal palace forts at Delhi and Agra, it was the setting for court life and ceremonial. Some courtyards were located along the ramparts, to collect the breezes. Water was precious, and the reflecting ponds in the Paien Bagh (*zenana*) are shallow, although there are many finely carved fountain basins. Planting areas are barely lower than the adjacent paths, and changes of level are generally minor. There is extensive use of marble and sandstone, although brick forms some platforms and tanks as well as paths, where it is laid in hexagonal pattern. Among the flowers were iris, stock and marigold. Fruit was in profusion, and included apples, oranges, lemons, grapes, figs, quinces, pomegranates, peaches and almonds. During the extensive dry season, plants were watered by hand.

195   Spray from the fountain once glistened on the scalloped bowl of this carved marble basin in the fort.

Plan 38   The fort, Lahore. As at Delhi and Agra, the Diwan-i-Am (A) leads into spacious courtyards – the larger (B) known as Jahangir's Quadrangle, the smaller (C) as Shah Jahan's. Beyond the latter is the Diwan-i-Khas (D), and further west the Moti Masjid, or Pearl Mosque (E).

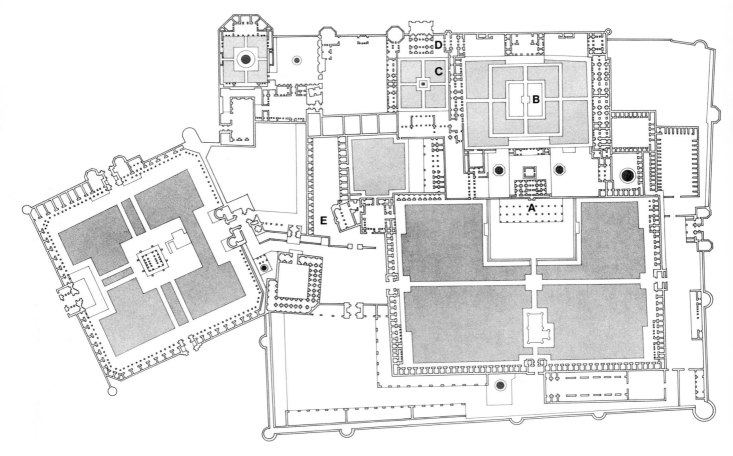

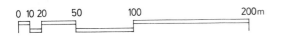

0 10 20   50   100   200m

196 Courtyard of stone and marble, using concentric circles and squares, near the Shah Bagh pavilion in the fort at Lahore.

197 Families enjoying the shade and water of a quadrangle in the fort at Lahore. Gardens within the forts are defined by buildings. Here a large open space contains a reservoir, with causeways as links to a central platform. The surrounding areas are lower so that water can flow down into them.

Shalamar Bagh
Lahore
Pakistan

198 A view of the Shalamar Bagh, Lahore, from the *zenana* terrace. Trees and sky are reflected in the water of the central reservoir that forms the focus of the garden between the upper and lower section.

The completion of the canal in the 17th century that brought the water of the Ravi River to Lahore prompted Shah Jahan to establish a garden to mark the occasion. Designed by the Emperor's architect and engineer, Ali Mardan Khan, the Shalamar Bagh's three terraces followed the traditional pattern of a Mughal garden, but its size made it truly royal. The first and third terraces are subdivided in *char bagh* formation; the second terrace, although much smaller, contains a reservoir that is the main focus of the garden and belies its size. This has more than one hundred fountains, whose spray cooled the air before the Emperor's white marble platform. This in turn was set over a water course at the foot of a white marble *chadar*. The drop between each terrace is punctuated by pavilions. The present structures are brick and plaster restorations, since the garden suffered great damage during the 18th century, when quantities of marble were reportedly taken to Amritsar. The reservoir, which has another carved platform at its centre linked by a causeway to the east and west sides, has an indented edge. Between the second and third terrace is a set of carved niches (*chini-kanas*).

Among the trees found in the garden are cypress, sycamore, mulberry and almond; fruits are apple, orange, apricot, quince, peach, plum, mango and cherry; flowers are

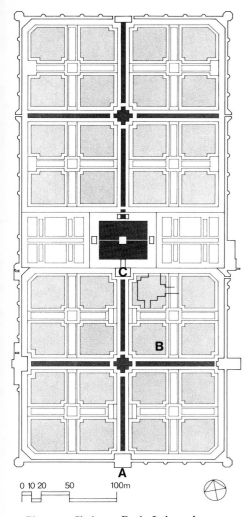

narcissus, iris, tulip and jasmine. The brickwork of the paths and pattern of the parterres follow local custom. The garden is contained behind a brick wall. Originally the entry to the garden followed the usual procedure, and was placed at the lowest level, where the visitor was faced by the cascades, and the garden revealed itself in stages, with the *zenana* garden at the highest level. The entry has now been transposed, and from the pavilion on the *zenana* terrace the whole garden is seen at once. Today, although the lower level channels are often empty, the garden is maintained in good condition and frequented by the public.

Plan 39 Shalamar Bagh, Lahore, has a classic plan with entry (A) in the south and two symmetrical gardens on either side of a central pool. The original *zenana* terrace (B) culminated in a pavilion (C) overlooking the water, which has its own stone bridge and platform.

199 The Emperor seated on his platform once enjoyed the cooled air and sound of water as it flowed through the pavilion at the level of the *zenana* terrace, down the chute, across a shallow pool and under the *chabutra* into the central reservoir.

200 Detail of the marble elaboration surrounding the central reservoir at Shalamar Bagh. Paths, paved with brick traditional to Lahore, are raised at a level higher than that of the adjacent parterres.

201 This enclosed space is designed for a cascade to pour over the miniature carved niches and link the level of the central reservoir to that of the third and lowest terrace, which leads from the archway on the right. A detail of the niches is seen in plate 101.

Tomb of Jahangir
Lahore
Pakistan

Located at Shah-Dara by the Ravi River near Lahore, the tomb and garden were set out during Jahangir's lifetime by the Empress Nur Jahan. The large enclosure is entered from the west, leading from a rectangular *caravanserai* that contains a mosque. The garden is divided into sixteen squares, the area of the mausoleum platform approximately equal to one of them. The red sandstone tomb, with its four corner minarets, is located at the very centre of the garden. It does not possess a central domed structure, but seems to require one. On all sides are raised causeways and tanks, from

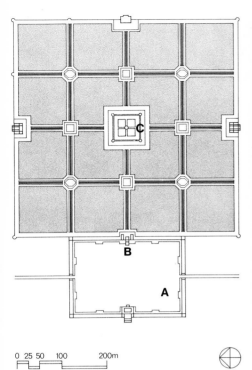

Plan 40   The Tomb of Jahangir, Lahore, is built close to a *caravanserai* (A) from which it was entered (B). In accordance with tradition, the mausoleum (C) stands in the centre of a garden divided symmetrically into four and then further subdivided.

202   View along an axis of the garden of the Tomb of Jahangir, Lahore. We are looking from an archway of the mausoleum platform towards one of the tanks that mark the junctions of the raised causeways.

which chutes and channels led water into the garden. Traditional to Lahore is the extensive use of brick, and the paths contain many patterns. There are cypress and palm trees, grassed areas and flower beds that display tulips, roses, lilies, poppies, violets, cyclamen and anemones. Jahangir loved flowers, and these were represented in inlay on the walls of his tomb. It is an imposing garden, its strict geometry an elaboration of the *char bagh* plan. It receives a number of visitors and is well maintained.

Pinjore near Chandigarh

This garden, a little over twelve miles from Chandigarh on the road to Simla, was built during the reign of the Emperor Aurangzeb by the Mughal general, Fadai Khan. It is located near a perennial spring, and sited to obtain a view of the hills across a fertile valley. The usual Mughal plan is here reversed, and entry is at the level of the uppermost terrace, with a view down the dominant main canal. Fountains were placed down the centre, and pathways, parterres and palm trees flank the canal, while orchards of mangoes are found on each side. From the highest level, the water passes under a pavilion and falls over a series of *chini-kanas* which held lamps. There are also *chadars*, since the gradient of the site allows the water to fall down a series of major changes of level. In the middle of a large reservoir on the sixth terrace is a water palace. It is surrounded by fountains, and connected to the banks via causeways.

Further gardens were created after Pinjore but the quality of their design deteriorated. Even this garden exhibits Sikh influence, and its scale is no longer intimate; it was the last of the great Mughal series.

203 The springs of Panchpura where the garden at Pinjore is situated prove a natural and inexhaustible source of water. This is a late Mughal garden, and its detailing no longer captures the charm achieved by its predecessors.

Facing page
204 At the lower end of this garden is a great variety of planting, and there are many fruit trees. Such trees were originally much more prevalent in the Islamic garden than they are today.

180

Fatehpur Sikri near Agra

This is a red sandstone city of palaces and courtyards less than twenty-five miles south-west of Agra. It was built by Akbar in the mid-16th century in less than a decade, and was located at the Shrine of Salim Chishti, who had foretold the birth of Akbar's son. Surrounded on three sides by a wall, with an artificial lake on the fourth, the complex contains a large mosque, a mausoleum, audience halls and a treasury, as well as palaces and their attendant buildings. Akbar was open to Hinduism as well as to Islam, and Rajputs were among his architects. This could well be one of the reasons why the buildings at Fatehpur Sikri are seemingly located at random when compared to the disciplined layout of the mosque court.

Many gardens and courtyards were laid out. Originally they and the buildings were served by an elaborate scheme of water supply involving wells, storage tanks, aqueducts and conduits. A number of wells were fed by the artificial lake, and two large reservoirs were built near the palaces. Water was raised by a system of wheels reputedly invented by Akbar himself, and was directed to the various channels, pools, fountains and outlets. Hot and cold water flowed into the baths (*hammams*).

At the sides of the large quadrangle near the Diwan-i-Am there are stone rings that were used to fasten canvas sheets that protected the audience from the sun. Other quadrangles have sunken water reservoirs, and gardens have shallow water courses. Abandoned eighteen years after they were begun, these hilltop buildings have survived in exceptional condition, and are a fitting tribute to the energy and ability of the most powerful, able and tolerant of the Mughal Emperors.

181

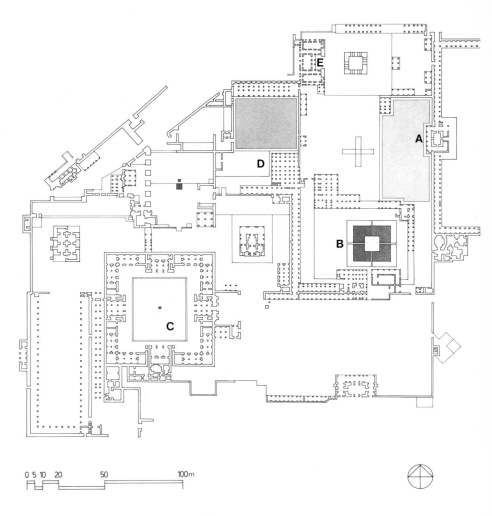

Plan 41 Akbar's capital of Fatehpur Sikri, a planned city built on a virgin site. Its elements form an ordered yet informal sequence from the Diwan-i-Am (A) to the Emperor's private apartments (B) with its pool and platform, the Jodh Bai Palace (C), Panch Mahal (D) and Diwan-i-Khas (E).

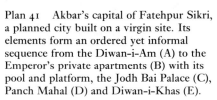

205 A platform within a square tank in front of what was possibly Akbar's Day Palace at Fatehpur Sikri. The Emperor seems to have been strongly influenced by the bridge concept, both as reality and as a symbol; a bridge over a water-filled sunken floor occurs again in his adjacent rest chamber.

182

**Tomb of Akbar
Sikandra**

This mausoleum near Agra was begun in the early years of the 17th century by Akbar and completed by Jahangir. The walls of the garden are surmounted by battlements, and there are octagonal towers in the corners. In the centre of each of these peripheral walls is a great gateway, although only one of these is genuine, the others being placed for symmetry.

The garden is based on the *char bagh* plan. Each quarter is divided by a high sandstone causeway with a shallow runnel down its centre. The causeway is of sufficient height to justify at regular intervals a link with the ground by a *chadar*, with steps on each side. Water once flowed down these chutes into small basins at the bottom, and from there irrigated the garden. At the outer edge of the causeway are red sandstone rings which once possibly held poles, with sockets at ground level, for the purpose of sheltering the causeway with awnings.

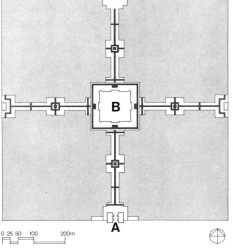

Plan 42   The Tomb of Akbar at Sikandra. Set within the traditional four-fold division, the entrance is to the south (A), with canals and causeways radiating in the cardinal directions from the central mausoleum (B).

206   View from the Tomb of Akbar at Sikandra towards the entry gateway. Narrow channels lead from a tank which breaks the perspective.

183

207 View across the large garden from the mausoleum building. This is one of the quarters formed by the *char bagh* plan.

Two-thirds of the way along the length of each causeway is a tank, and there is a further tank at the centre of each side of the platform surrounding the tomb. In the centre of each tank is a fountain. Various wells in the garden supplied water for the fountains and channels, as well as for irrigation; pressure was achieved through overhead tanks.

Today no water flows along the channels, fills the tanks or bubbles from the fountains. The broad expanses of paving that could support a colourful procession are bare. But the sandstone and marble tomb maintains its dignity and quietude, and the design of the surrounding garden still carries the same assurance intended by its original designer. It is well maintained, and many visitors to Agra on their way to or from Fatehpur Sikri stop here.

208 From the tomb's four raised causeways water flows down *chadars* into small basins from which it irrigates the garden.

209 The Jag Niwas Palace at Udaipur is now a luxury hotel with marble rooms and stained glass windows. There are several courtyards. This ornamental pool, in which a fountain gently plays, was built in the last century.

**Lake Palaces
Udaipur**

Udaipur was built as a local capital in the mid-16th century. There are several lakes in the vicinity, and Lake Pichola, set among the hills, has two island palaces. Jag Mandir is the smaller, and Shah Jahan lived there for a while, amid its gardens and many balconies, when in rebellion against his father. Although Mughal in style, there is a strong Rajput influence, and the palace buildings now mostly date from the 18th century. They exhibit a fascinating contrast of ordered geometry within a highly picturesque setting. The Jag Niwas Palace is now the Lake Palace Hotel, and with its history, present-day luxury and romanticism bears comparison with Isfahan's Shah Abbas Hotel, which was once a *caravanserai*.

Plan 43 Plan of the ornamental pool at Udaipur, seen in a photograph above, one of the most ornate of Islamic curvilinear designs in which land and water mingle.

0 1 2   5   10m

210 The island palace of Jag Mandir, with Lake Pichola beyond and Udaipur itself in the distance.

Other regions

IN ORDER THAT ITS MESSAGE should be clear, the Quran portrayed images that were familiar and analogies that were easily understood. It is therefore probable that the Islamic image of paradise was based on the nature of gardens existing at the time – gardens that were known to be agreeable and pleasurable. In other words, the Islamic garden was based less on a particular theory or doctrine than on the achievement of comfort and occasionally prestige; subsequently, it was on these pleasure gardens that the idea of the paradise garden was based. An attractive story relates to a very large and beautiful garden in the early days of Islam. The owner, Abu-Talha, was praying there one day under a tree when he became distracted by its beauty. So that in future he would think of nothing but God, he went to Mohammed and offered his garden for the use and enjoyment of the public.

Characteristic features of gardens in several regions are described below. These attributes were not always necessarily unique to a particular location, but they were certainly always associated with that region.

North Africa and Sicily

Gardens in the Islamic tradition first appeared in the Maghrib in 9th-century Tunis. Sultans owned gardens which they used for pleasure and amusement, as well as orchards from which they sold the fruit. The gardens and courtyards of this region, including Morocco, may be divided into two categories. The first was the large garden, the *arsa*, or *aguedal*, of the wealthy, geometrically laid out in a series of squares which were irrigated successively. Often these gardens were terraced. They were not primarily decorative, although pavilions overlooked the plantations and surrounding countryside. Sometimes groups of gardens located away from the dense centre of a city formed a park that covered many hectares.

The gardens were planted with flowers chosen for their fragrance rather than their appearance; for this reason there were no geraniums, as their perfume was considered to be unpleasant. A trellis would support jasmine and Bougainvillaea. There were a few selected types of fruit trees: oranges, lemons, mandarins, figs, apples, pears and plums, as well as pomegranates, apricots, bananas and quince. The fruit trees were planted in regular formation, but were not pruned, and so obscured light from any vegetation at their base. Other trees were cypress, laurel, mulberry and olive. Vegetables included peppers, aubergines, potatoes, cabbages, marrows and pimentos; sugar-cane, mint, sage and sweet marjoram were also grown. The flowers and fruit supplied the royal households, and were also grown for sale. A further role of the large garden was as a location for the harem. It was also used as a place of recreation, when mint tea was drunk under the fruit trees. Ample lakes, fed from streams, contained pleasure boats, a feature also found in some of the larger royal gardens in Iran.

Water that supplied the garden was often drawn from a well by clay pots, or raised from a river by a water wheel turned by a mule; the sound of the wheel creaking no doubt accompanied the bubbling of the water and song of the blackbirds and goldfinches. The water that irrigated the garden was confined by raised paths. Among the plants, earth was built in low banks, and the gardener with his hoe would direct the water to the various straight-edged plots.

The second type of enclosed space was more a town patio, a *riadh*, or large formal area, enclosed on two or more sides by galleries and comparable to the courtyards found in Andalusia. Outside was the traffic, the dust and the bustle of the street; inside was quiet and repose. The scent of flowers and the sound of birds proclaimed this protected space, the first view of which was often from a niche or other opening off axis. Paths crossed the patio at right angles, their intersection marked by a pavilion or fountain. These paths were surfaced with marble, ceramic tile or enamelled brick, all of which provided a cool surface. Sometimes there were channels. Tile decoration was confined to panels on the surrounding walls. Fruit trees and flowers could also be present. In later patios, there were brightly painted kiosks and balustrades of wrought-iron. Undoubtedly, the forerunner of the Moroccan patio was to be found in Iran; the model was quite appropriate, and the tradition has continued.`

To the east of Morocco, the outskirts of Algiers boasted many luxurious country houses. These were renowned for their elaborate and carefully maintained gardens. Oranges, lemons and roses abounded, and marble paving defined channels in which ran warm as well as cold water. On a grander scale was the 11th-century Qala of the Bani Hammad. A very large, irregular, walled enclosure, entered through a domed portal, contained a central palace complex with inner and outer reception halls, several courtyards and a straight-sided lake. Dwellings in Ifriqiya (today's Tunisia) contained courtyards the design of which was influenced by refugees from Andalusia. The skillful use of irrigation shown by the Moors was put to use in the North African towns and gardens. Water from the surrounding higher elevations was brought to the urban areas via underground canals, and wells were also used. The centre of Umayyad Ifriqiya was Qairawan, established in the latter half of the 7th century. Its 9th-century Great Mosque covers a large area, and was possibly a model for subsequent mosques in the Maghrib.

Muslims immigrated to Sicily from the Maghrib at the beginning of the 10th century. Coming from an arid country, they were pleased to see the quantity of water available on the island. Palermo was well supplied with water from its two rivers, the Papireto and the Kemonia, as well as from many springs. Water was the fountain of life, and once again the Moors introduced new techniques of irrigation for crops. Water was also a source of pleasure for body and spirit. Accordingly, public baths were built, villas were adorned with cascades, pools and fishponds and fountains graced courtyards.

In the second half of the 11th century, the Normans took over Sicily, but a strong Islamic influence was to remain in arts and crafts, particularly textiles, ivory carving and mosaics. Any surviving architecture dates from this Arab-Norman period, chiefly in the form of small palaces and pavilions. In gardens and courtyards, the creation of fountains was popular, evolving from generation to generation. In the course of time, many fountains were abandoned; a few have been restored.

As did many other nations and cultures, the early Egyptians ascribed a most attractive picture to life after death. The image portrayed in contemporary records was of a garden containing green plants, running water and fruit for the picking.

The Egyptian house and garden was customarily surrounded by rows of palms mixed with other planting; the purpose was to mark a garden's boundaries, stabilize its soil and provide shade. Trees of different types and heights enabled the sunlight to penetrate to the ground, where low-level planting could grow in a changing pattern of light and shade. Vegetation also reduced the dust and, to some extent, regulated humidity and lowered the temperature. Although houses were located close together, a system of roof ventilation caught the cool air from the small patios. No very early gardens remain, but contemporary drawings show varieties of trees, vines, pools and occasional enclosures for animals.

When the Nile valley flooded, water poured over the cultivated area and into holding ponds further back from the river; during the dry season, water was raised from the river, often through a wheel turned by a bullock, and retained in smaller artificial pools; there was an ample supply of mud. Accordingly, many houses outside the dense urban core were surrounded by gardens. These usually took the form of orchards, with rows of palm trees, pools containing papyrus and lotus and vineyards. Records also depicted pleasure gardens, with pools and boats.

Cairo, founded in the latter half of the 10th century, contained many gardens, public as well as private. There were also several garden palaces, which reputedly boasted not only many roses but also trees of gold and lakes with silver gondolas. The palace courtyards of the Sultans reflected their power, and a succession of formal rectangular courtyards contributed to the atmosphere of grandeur. Courtyards rather than gardens also form today's chief legacy, since in a harsh dry climate stone survives where planting does not. The early Islamic courtyards that remain belong for the most part to mosques and are often completely paved, with ablution facilities in the centre.

A few of the courtyards in older private houses can still be seen. The North Africans' love of nature was shown by their large courtyards, which allowed plenty of light to reach the trees and flowers. Even the poorest had a plant in some container, or the occasional tree, perhaps with a bird singing in its cage. Notwithstanding the birdsong, the courtyard maintained its traditional role as a place of escape, for quiet meditation and contemplation. There was always a water basin and flowers. Architecturally, owing to the loose aggregation of rooms, customary in Egyptian domestic planning, these courtyards played a key role in holding together and unifying the total concept. Their paved paths, limited vegetation and marble fountains, sometimes bordered by a colonnade, also provided a view and cool air for the surrounding dwelling. Many houses in Cairo were of several storeys, and planting was even found on the roof. It is recounted that a calf was once taken up to a roof, where it grew up into a bull, at which time it was employed to turn a water wheel.

On the Arabian peninsula rainfall is very scarce indeed. However, it falls irregularly in the south and west, and assisted by dams in these areas, particularly in the Yemen, there was the strongest possibility for the early cultivation of gardens, including elaborate terracing. There was ample ground water in the oases, there were a number of artesian wells and in several areas, such as the Oman peninsula, there were great palm gardens. What gardens there were would have been influenced by Egyptian, Mesopotamian and

Iranian precedents. The city of Riyadh's name (meaning garden) implies that there were gardens in the vicinity, and thus the presence of water. At one time, gardens may have existed there in profusion, but today there is little trace or even descriptive record of gardens dating from earlier periods.

In Syria, irrigated areas intensively cultivated by rural communities working co-operatively were termed a garden, or *ghuta*. In the midst of arid land, they were located near one or more springs, from which water supplied canals. Subsistence for villagers and their animals was provided through a closed economy. Vegetables and fruit were grown near the source of water, the intensity of cultivation and tree planting decreasing further from the source; fields with vines and cereals were located on the periphery. Muslim tradition regarded the *ghuta* of Damascus (Dimashk), whose gardens and orchards surrounded the former Umayyad capital, as an earthly paradise, and a possible location of the original Garden of Eden.

Visiting Damascus at the end of the 12th century, Ibn Jubayr, a Spanish Muslim traveller described the city:

> The gardens encircle it like the halo round the moon and contain it as it were the calyx of a flower. To the east, its green Ghuta stretches as far as the eye can see, and wherever you look on its four sides its ripe fruits hold the gaze. By Allah, they spoke truth who said, 'If Paradise be on earth it is Damascus without a doubt; and if it be in Heaven, Damascus is its earthly counterpart and equivalent.

Turkey The early nomadic Turks roamed over areas where nature was harsh and demanded respect. Dispersing from Central Asia, they carried with them an image of a place where the climate would be mild and game abundant. The idea of a garden, with its implications of leisure, was introduced to them by various sedentary peoples. Gardens they subsequently built reflected both the early respect for nature and the particular culture of the area. When Islam reached Turkey in the 10th century, a new harmonious relationship between man and nature was introduced. Here, as elsewhere in the *Dar-al-Islam*, the concept of the paradise garden was easily accepted; nonetheless, courtyards, pools, canals, fountains and coloured glass mosaic had already been used in gardens before the introduction of Islamic garden concepts. Soon after Islam was introduced, Turks became involved in the government and defence of the Islamic world, from Spain to the Arabian Sea. It may be assumed that they then both influenced other nations and received from them cultural ideas, design concepts and garden practices.

Sources that describe the early garden in Turkey are rare. Only a few miniatures and a very small number of contemporary descriptions by native writers and foreign travellers are available; but some old palaces with their gardens survived for a longer period of time, and from these some concepts may be gathered. The palaces were built in favourable climatic locations, and their gardens used, as in Iran, for affairs of state as well as for informal dining and entertaining. Sometimes outdoor living was so important that the site for the garden, in relation to its beauty, view, air and water, would be chosen before the requirements for the building were met. A place with a view over water was highly desirable, or, in Istanbul and along the coast, a garden kiosk overlooking the sea. For this reason, the Turkish Islamic garden was possibly less determined by axes and architectural climax than its counterparts elsewhere, especially when Islam became more divorced from Arabic culture and local customs predominated. Nonetheless, the garden was still ordered, and besides kiosks there was an extensive use of pools, canals and fountains and many flowers, often of a single species. These characteristics applied to both large and small gardens, and also to courtyards.

As the Ottomans extended their territory, further palaces were built, and their large gardens divided into courts containing pavilions or kiosks, with hunting grounds on the periphery. The Topkapi Saray on the site of the old Acropolis of Byzantium was the residence of the Sultans from the 16th to the 19th century, and its construction took place over an extended period. The vast complex included apartments, offices, schools and libraries, and its gardens overlooking the sea contained numerous pavilions as well as vineyards and orchards, basins and fountains. However, the garden design was not completely in the Islamic tradition, since the climate rendered irrigation unnecessary.

By the beginning of the 18th century, the Ottoman Empire had already reached its greatest extent, and extravagant practices were common. Many banquets were held in the popular tulip gardens, often at night, and there are descriptions of candles carried on the backs of turtles that moved among the tulip beds, while caged nightingales sang from the trees. Eventually the empire dissolved, and gardens, along with several other artistic attributes, declined.

Uzbekistan   Garden design and techniques were well advanced in Central Asia by the 14th and 15th centuries. Under the Timurids, the area of cultivable land was increased through the development of irrigation, and gardens flourished in Herat in Afghanistan, and Samarkand in Uzbekistan. Samarkand was located in a plain. The town was surrounded by forests, orchards, vineyards and grazing land. Within this green belt, which was a characteristic feature of many cities of the region, including Iran, there were gardens and palaces, for which rivers and streams supplied adequate water. Clavijo, a Spaniard who led the embassy from Henry III, King of Castile and León in the 15th century, wrote that the gardens and vineyards surrounding Samarkand were so numerous 'that a traveller approaching the city sees only a hilly mount of trees, and the houses embowered among them remain invisible'.

The plan of the Samarkand garden reflected the Iranian tradition of the paradise garden. Shut off from the outside world, it was peaceful, green, shady and fragrant. It was also geometrical, axial and formal. A pavilion, standing on a platform, would be located at the junction of the major and secondary axes that divided the garden. A canal led down the centre of the garden. A central pool, fountains and cascades further enhanced the role played by water. Shallow channels were faced with blue tiles. From magnificent arched entries, major views were directed towards focal points on the main axis, and this orientation was reinforced by high enclosing walls and dense peripheral planting. Gardens located on hillsides or on river and canal banks contained flat straight-sided terraces; these were supported by retaining walls, and linked by steps or ramps.

Shade, decoration and the use of the garden determined the choice of planting. Trees, among which were cypress, elm, plane, poplar, sycamore and willow, were highly regarded, and rows and groupings were composed of one particular species. Flowers were laid out in regular beds, and included amaranthus, calendulas, cornflowers, lilacs, lilies and, especially, tulips, carnations, hyacinths and many roses. There were also mulberries and nuts; vineyards and orchards completed the picture. Clavijo is reported to have

191

described one location at Samarkand as 'a large garden with many different shade and fruit trees. It contained basins and skilfully laid-out lawns, and there was so wide a space by the garden entrance that many people could take delight in sitting here in summertime, by the water and under the trees'. There is another description of a garden in Samarkand, this time by Babur, on a visit to the *char bagh* of Darwesh Muhammad Tarkan. 'It lies overlooking the whole of Qulba Meadow', he wrote, on the slope below the Bagh-i Maydan. Moreover it is arranged symmetrically, terrace above terrace, and is planted with beautiful narwan and cypresses and white poplar. A most agreeable sojourning place, its one defect is the want of a large stream.' Elsewhere Clavijo described the garden of the residence where he was staying:

> We found it to be enclosed by a high wall which in its circuit may measure a full league around, and within it is full of fruit trees of all kinds save only limes and citron-trees which we noted to be lacking. Further, there are here six great tanks, for throughout the orchard is conducted a great system of water, passing from end to end: while leading from one tank to the next they have planted five avenues of trees, very lofty and shady, which appear as streets for they are paved to be like platforms. These quarter the orchard in every direction, and off the five main avenues other smaller roads are led to variegate the plan . . . In the exact centre there is a hill, built up artificially of clay brought hither by hand; it is very high and its summit is a small level space that is enclosed by a palisade of wooden stakes.
>
> Within this enclosure are built several very beautiful palaces, each with its complement of chambers magnificently ornamented in gold and blue, the walls being panelled with tiles of these and other colours. This mound on which the palaces have been built is encircled below by deep ditches that are filled with water, for a runlet from the main stream brings this water which flows into these ditches with a continuous and copious supply. To pass up unto this hillock to the level of the palaces they have made two bridges, one on the other part, the other opposite . . . . There are to be seen many deer which Timur has caused to be caught and brought hither, and there are pheasants here in great abundance.

One highly visible component of these royal gardens was the tents used for celebrations and receptions. Circular in shape, they were rich and colourful, and were made of red cloth and embroidered silk. They were supported by poles within the canvas walls, rather than by stays. In addition, there were awnings tied with cord to wooden poles, which caught the breezes and provided shade.

Eventually, from the 17th century, political instability in Central Asia contributed to the decline both of the gardens located there and of the gardening tradition that had supported them. However, the gardens of private houses still maintained some of the principles on which they had been based.

Afghanistan An account of the garden in Afghanistan is provided by Babur. Familiar from his youth with the famous gardens of Samarkand, he was determined to introduce such ideas as he progressed south. Kabul itself was described by Babur as 'a scenery of mountains and valleys, wilderness and gardens, so beautiful that the realization of this beauty completely satisfies human taste'.

The 'Garden of Fidelity' (Bagh-i Wafa), constructed by Babur at the very beginning of the 16th century, was about fifty miles from Kabul on rising ground overlooking the Kabul River, and is described in his memoirs:

I laid out the Four-gardens, known as the Bagh-i Wafa, on a rising-ground, facing south. There oranges, citrons and pomegranates grew in abundance. . . . I had plaintains brought and planted there; they did very well. . . . The garden lies high, has running-water close at hand, and a mild winter climate. In the middle of it, a one-mill stream flows constantly past the little hill on which are the four garden-plots. In the south-west part of it there is a reservoir, ten by ten, round which are orange trees and a few pomegranates, the whole encircled by a trefoil-meadow. This is the best part of the garden, a most beautiful sight when the oranges take colour. Truly that garden is admirably situated!

Later, on a march to India, Babur was to write about the same garden: 'Those were the days of the garden's beauty; its lawns were one sheet of trefoil; its pomegranate trees yellowed to autumn splendour, their fruit full red; fruit on the orange trees green and glad . . . the pomegranates were excellent.'

There were also other gardens with which this imperial gardener was involved. The 'Large Garden' (Bagh-i Kala) was located on a hillside outside Kabul. There were many natural streams, and Babur's first concern was that one should be straightened to form the axis of his garden and supply its fountains. The regular geometrical plan of the Islamic garden followed.

Babur was involved not only in the design of his gardens, but in the choice of plants as well. He made lists of wild flowers, is reported to have noted thirty-one species of tulips in the Kabul area and ordered specific trees, shrubs and flowers to be planted in Kabul's streets and squares. When describing the Bagh-i Maydan in Herat, Babur mentions the 'wondrous flower-beds, with yellow and red flowers blooming in clusters, while others are of red only, and in some both are mixed together, as though scattered'.

He also collected and experimented with fruits and flowers that he received from foreign lands. It was the Emperor Babur's knowledge of plants and his regard for the order and symmetry of the Islamic garden that he eventually introduced into India.

Bardo Palace
Algiers Algeria

211 Fountain in a courtyard of the Bardo Palace in Algiers. The focus on water, marble paving, arcades and planting continues the earlier tradition, but the more casual placing of architectural elements such as windows and doors reflects a later relaxation of axial planning.

The summer residence of Governor Mustafa was erected at the turn of the 18th century in a high part of the city of Algiers overlooking the harbour. It is in an area that was once outside the city boundary, containing many attractive residences surrounded by orchards and gardens, with a profusion of trees and flowers. The residence subsequently became one of several annexes of the Summer Palace, and is now a museum. There are several courtyards with polychrome faience and marble paving, as well as white walls that contrast with the green of the surrounding luxuriant foliage. There are also fountains, forming the focus of the courtyard in which they stand, and of the loggia within which they are sheltered.

---

al-Seheimy House
Cairo
Egypt

Built around a courtyard, this house has many Islamic characteristics. Walls in the northern wing are tiled, there are carved wood screens in the windows and the profusely planted garden has a quadripartite plan, with a pool at the centre crossing of the paths. Located near the Khan al-Khalili bazaar, entry is through a small passage at a level lower than the street outside, and this area shields the inner court from curious gazes. The house and its courtyard are well preserved and maintained.

212 View through to the
courtyard of the al-
Seheimy House in Cairo.
The house is near the
busy market, but the
courtyard, which is
divided into four by
pathways with a fountain
in the centre, turns in
upon itself for seclusion
and privacy.

213 Another view of the al-Seheimy House, Cairo, looking
through a screen that is typical of carved woodwork found
elsewhere in North Africa.

Ibn Tulun Mosque
Cairo
Egypt

This 9th-century mosque is of brick faced with stucco. It is a very fine monument,
impressive in its simplicity, but has undergone many a restoration and reconstruction.
It is separated from the street on three sides by an outer court (*ziyada*) which extends
its size even further. Surrounding the large inner square courtyard is an arcade, its
porportions of solid and void mutually balancing. The pointed arches are among the
earliest known. Within the courtyard is a domed structure with a basin for ritual
ablutions at its centre, dating from the end of the 13th century. The mosque is also known
as al-Qatai.

214 Courtyard of the ancient Ibn Tulun
Mosque in Cairo. The domed structure in
the centre contains an ablution basin.
Behind the arcade with its early example of
the pointed arch is a spiral minaret, much
restored.

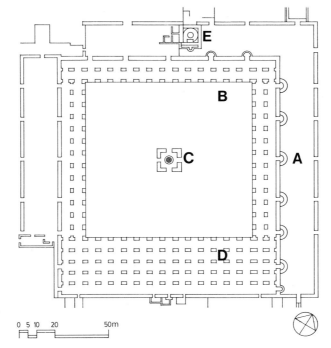

Plan 44 The Ibn Tulun Mosque, Cairo.
Protected by its *ziyada*, or outer court (A),
the mosque is like an Islamic house in
turning its back upon the outside world and
concentrating upon its courtyard (B) and
ablution fountain (C). The mosque (D) faces
Mecca. On the opposite side is its spiral
minaret (E).

**Sultan Hassan
Mosque
Cairo
Egypt**

This large college and mosque complex, with its fortress-like and sober character, is a masterpiece of 14th-century Mamluk architecture, balanced and majestic. It consists of four immense *iwans*, serving as oratories and auditoria, in cruciform plan around an inner court; there are also colleges, with their attached residences, and, towards the south, the tomb of the Sultan surmounted by a vast cupola. In contrast to the entry passage and surrounding recesses, the courtyard forms a great well of light. In the middle of the geometrically patterned floor is a covered fountain, its octagonal base roofed by a dome.

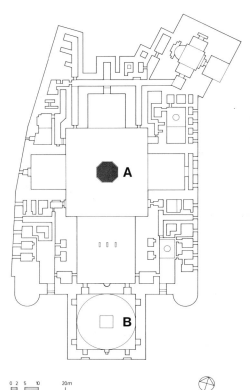

0 2 5 10   20m

Plan 45   The Sultan Hassan Mosque, Cairo. Hemmed in by the surrounding buildings, the mosque and its courtyard (A), with *iwans* on three sides and ablution fountain in the centre, is dominated by the huge domed tomb of the Sultan (B).

215   Light streams into the majestic courtyard of the Sultan Hassan Mosque. In its centre is a domed, octagonal ablution basin, while on each side is a great *iwan*.

198

Bulkawara Palace
Samarra
Iraq

The Bulkawara Palace was built in the mid-9th century and provides an early Muslim example of the *char bagh*. Running through the centre of the large complex was a strong axis, off which several courtyards followed the *char bagh* concept. Some ruined walls are all that remain.

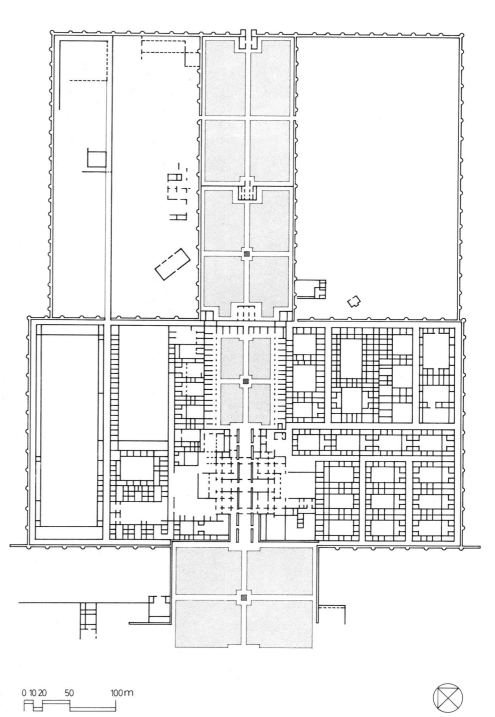

Plan 46   The Bulkawara Palace, Samarra, now in ruins. The four gardens and courtyards, lying along the central axis, all are divided into the traditional four-fold *char bagh*.

0 10 20   50   100 m

**Attarine Medersa
Fez
Morocco**

Built in the 14th century by Sultan Abu Said Uthman, this college is reached by a narrow passage from the street. In the courtyard, overlooked by students' rooms with their cedarwood grilles, are columns and capitals of carved stone, engraved stucco work and calligraphy, carved wood and mosaic tile. The scale of the carving and patterns is very intricate throughout. In the centre of the courtyard is a fountain, spilling over into a recess just below the level of the paving.

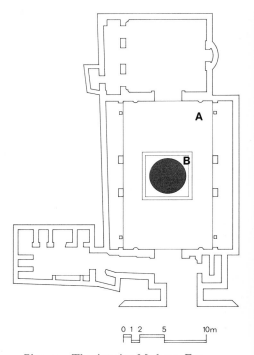

0 1 2   5   10m

Plan 47   The Attarine Medersa, Fez, clustered round its courtyards (A) and circular fountain (B).

216   Fountain basin in the courtyard of the Attarine Medersa. Elaborately carved cedar frames the doorway beyond, while a band of calligraphy separates the coloured mosaic-tile base of the wall from the carved stucco above.

Bou Inaniye Medersa
Fez
Morocco

This college was built in the mid-14th century for prayer and instruction, and followed the customary pattern of providing a series of student rooms at an upper level, which overlooked a courtyard. It is a fine example of Merinid architecture, with mosaic dados, carved plaster, cedarwood friezes and a marble-paved courtyard, in the centre of which is a simple flat basin.

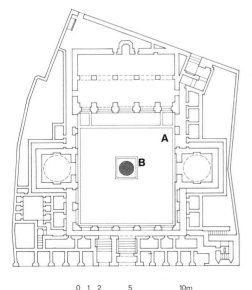

217 Low fountain basin set within the paved courtyard of the Bou Inaniye Medersa, Fez. The materials are characteristically rich: carved cedarwood, stucco, and coloured mosaic tile for the surrounding walls, stone and marble for the paving.

Plan 48 The Bou Inaniye Medersa, Fez – again the courtyard (A) with its fountain (B) flanked by *iwans*.

0 1 2   5   10m

201

Dar Batha Palace
Fez
Morocco

This is a 19th-century building with a large courtyard, most of which is surrounded by an arcade. A small rectangular pool is flanked by two fountain basins, their overflow splashing into a star-shaped recess set in a mosaic-tiled surround. The courtyard as a whole is surfaced with stone and mosaic, and is partly shaded by trees. The Moorish tradition remains, but the scale and detailing are of a later culture.

218 Fountains in the courtyard of the Dar Batha Palace, Fez. The traditional focus on water, the use of mosaic and enclosing arcades have remained, but, by the 19th century, adherence to symmetry in the layout of the palace and its courtyard is no longer of major concern.

**Karaouyne Mosque
Fez
Morocco**

This very large mosque was founded in the mid-9th century. Established before the al-Azhar University of Cairo, it became an important Islamic centre of learning, a reputation which it still holds. It received continuous additions and alterations until well into the 12th century, with the further addition of two pavilions containing fountains as late as the 17th century. In common with many Hispano-Moresque mosques, most courtyards in Fez are wider than they are long, and the courtyard of the Karaouyne Mosque is entered near the centre of its width. The marble ablution basin in the centre of the tiled courtyard was installed at the beginning of the 13th century. The predominant colours here are enlivened by white, as distinct from the dark reds and brown of the *medersas*.

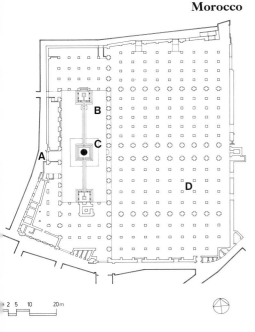

219   View into the courtyard of the Karaouyne Mosque, Fez, from a passageway in the *souk*. A carved marble ablution basin is set in the coloured tiled floor of the courtyard, while an elaborately decorated portal leads to the mosque beyond.

Plan 49   The Karaouyne Mosque, Fez, a 9th-century foundation with rigidly symmetrical layout. From the entrance (A) one enters a rectangular courtyard (B) centred upon the ablution fountain (C). The large and many-columned mosque (D) lies beyond.

Sahrij Medersa
Fez
Morocco

The Sahrij Medersa was built by Sultan Abu al-Hassan in the 14th century. Following the customary form for a theological seminary, its decoration is sumptuous, with polychrome faience, much carved wood and stucco work. In the centre of the courtyard is a flat rectangular basin, its calm, dark surface reflecting the surrounding elaborately treated surfaces.

220 Looking down from roof level into the courtyard of the Sahrij Medersa at Fez. Seen here is the full range of the materials customarily used in this period: tile, mosaic, stucco, carved wood and stone.

Facing page
221 The height of the two-storey enclosure ensures a constant degree of shadow for the small courtyard and central pool, in which the surrounding decorated surfaces are reflected.

204

222 The immense tank of the Aguedal Gardens, Morocco, across which pleasure boats once floated. The extensive gardens, the large body of water and the many shade trees provided strong contrast to the crowded city of Marrakesh near by.

Aguedal
Marrakesh
Morocco

This immense garden was laid out by the Almohads in the 12th century, although its present form was probably established by Abd ar-Rahman in the mid-19th century. It was surrounded by walls. Pools serve for irrigation, the largest of which was once used for pleasure boats. Its immense size provides welcome relief from the adjacent city, and is a delightful contrast to the surrounding dry countryside. There are many olive trees.

Bahia Palace and
Gardens
Marrakesh
Morocco

The sumptuously decorated Bahia Palace was designed at the end of the 19th century. The various palace courtyards, with their stone, stucco, and tiled surfaces, trap the dazzling sunlight. To the east, the palace garden is irrigated by water from a large square basin. There is an older spirit about this garden, which contains a variety of trees and much jasmine, and in contrast to the courtyards there are many cool dark places.

223 View through an iron screen to a
courtyard within the Bahia Palace,
Marrakesh. Like the Dar Batha Palace
courtyard (plate 218) this one focuses upon
the traditional fountain basin set in a
mosaic-tile surround.

224 Trees cast their shade over a path in the sunlit Mamounia Gardens in Marrakesh. Orange groves and vegetable gardens lie beyond.

Facing page
225 Elaborate decoration on the wall of the courtyard of the Medersa Ibn Youssef in Marrakesh. The multi-coloured faience dado, separated by two bands of calligraphy from the stucco above carved in flowing organic patterns, richly displays the wide range of the Islamic craftsman's resources.

Mamounia Gardens
Marrakesh
Morocco

Established in the 17th century, this somewhat neglected garden still contains orange groves and olive trees. It also provides the site for the famous hotel of the same name, and in addition now contains a pool, paved terraces and tennis courts, set in masses of vegetation.

Medersa Ibn Youssef
Marrakesh
Morocco

Originally established in the 14th century by the Merinid Sultan, Abu al-Hassan, this theological college was rebuilt in the mid-16th century by the Saadian, Moulay Abu Abdallah. The rectangular pool, with its run off channel, is at the level of the courtyard paving. Multicoloured mosaic lines the surrounding walls; above this is intricately carved plaster painted the customary red-brown, while doorway panels are of elaborately carved wood. It is one of the largest *medersas* in the Maghrib and at one time accommodated over one hundred pupils.

Tombs of the Saadian Rulers Marrakesh Morocco

Constructed under the Saadian sovereign, Ahmed al-Mansour al-Dehbi, in the late 16th century, these tombs contain the remains of most of the Saadian monarchs, as well as their wives and children. Within the mausoleum itself are columns of marble, stalactite arches, brightly coloured and geometrically patterned mosaic in good condition, as well as dark brown woodwork, handsomely carved. The adjacent burial ground has mosaic-tiled paths and a fountain basin. This area was sealed until its rediscovery at the beginning of this century, however, and may not originally have displayed the attractive flowers and grass now found there.

Bou Inaniye Medersa Meknès Morocco

This college was built during the reign of Sultan Abu al-Hassan in the mid-14th century, and has been recently restored. The tiled courtyard is entered from a corridor two storeys high, and contains a round ablution basin with a scalloped edge. There is a slight recess at floor level to take water spillage, but the tiled surface continues. Between the mosaic-tiled columns surrounding the courtyard are intricately carved wood screens. Overlooking the courtyard from a higher level, where the plaster work is finely carved, are the small rooms where the students lodged.

226 Marble fountain basin set in a crossing of coloured mosaic-tile paths in the garden of the Tombs of the Saadian Rulers in Marrakesh.

227 View from a window of one of the students' rooms to a courtyard of the Bou Inaniye Medersa, Meknès. The customary tilework, carved wood and elaborate stucco are seen beyond.

228 Basin within a shaped recess set in a tiled path in the Dar Jamai, Meknès. Pathways are characteristically raised above the planting areas. This garden dates from the last century, and its detailing fails to reach the standard set by the earlier work.

Dar Jamai
Meknès
Morocco

Although this palace dates from the late 19th century, it has a courtyard reflecting several traditional Islamic characteristics: tiled pathways, which are raised above the level of the planting, and luxuriant vegetation. Unfortunately, the detailing of the path edging and fountain basins is crude, and betrays the decline in garden and courtyard design which had already occurred by this time.

Tomb of Moulay Ismail
Meknès
Morocco

An elaborate gateway in an otherwise blank façade opens on a covered area containing a trickling fountain. A sunlit courtyard with a fountain, and an arcade at each end, leads from this. The third courtyard is enclosed, although light streams down from an upper level. It is colonnaded, and its mosaic-tiled floor and dado carry a far more elaborate pattern than the preceding courts. It commemorates a despot who died in the 18th century, and who was responsible for the building of many orchards, gardens and pleasure pavilions. The tomb is maintained in excellent condition.

229 Marble fountain-head and fluted basin in a courtyard of the Tomb of Moulay Ismail at Meknès.

Chellah Rabat Morocco

This district, just outside the city walls of Rabat, was originally established by the Romans, and building resumed in the 14th century. The area is surrounded by fortifications and entered through a monumental gateway. Amidst the gardens it now contains are tombs, a mosaic-faced minaret and a tank. Small channels lead from two fountain basins into the tank, which has an overflow channel. Mosaic once covered the tank surrounds, as well as adjacent wall surfaces. There are several storks' nests in the vicinity, adding to the overall attraction of these shaded green slopes on a hot afternoon.

230 Tank in a courtyard in Chellah, Rabat. Two fountain basins lead into the tank, and mosaic tile once covered most of the surrounding surfaces.

San Giovanni degli Eremiti Palermo Italy

Exhibiting Moorish influence, San Giovanni was established in the 12th century; the cloisters date from the 13th century. Even though built under the Normans, the Arab presence remains, particularly in the charming scale of the enclosure, with its luxuriant planting bounded by straight paths.

Topkapi Saray Istanbul Turkey

The Topkapi Palace (*Saray*) dates from the 15th to the 19th century. Built as the residence of the Sultans, and forming the most extensive example in existence of Ottoman civil architecture, the complex is composed of separate pavilions, or kiosks, set asymmetrically in courtyards and gardens amidst pools and fountains. There are several courtyards, each one related to a particular segment of the large community, which served the Emperor's supreme executive and judicial council as well as the palace.

The outer court was a general service area. Councils of state were held in the Diwan-i-Am, the second court, and there were also kitchens and stables in this area. Planted with cypress, it once contained several fountains. Although now tranquil, it was possibly once the scene of pageantry, when it would have been crowded with officials and guards on occasions of public business.

The third and fourth courts were the Sultan's private domain. Offices for court and government officials, the palace school, the Sultan's reception room and private apartments, as well as the harem surrounded the third court. A marble terrace with a pool links this court with the next. The fourth court is really a large enclosed garden at various levels. A stair beside a pool leads down into what was once a tulip garden and the site of tulip festivals in the first half of the 18th century. This garden also contains several pleasure kiosks. The outer, or fifth, court originally served the palace as a hunting and sports ground and contained flower, fruit and vegetable gardens. It is now part of a Europeanized park extending to the Golden Horn at Saray Point.

231 A small garden in Palermo, in the cloister of the convent of San Giovanni degli Eremiti. Many of the details are Christian, but the original spirit of the garden and the scale of its enclosure clearly derive from the Moors.

232 The Ottoman palace of the Topkapi in Instanbul is a varied collection of pavilions and kiosks, with domes and minarets rising above luxuriant plants and trees. This region receives more rain than many other parts of the Islamic world, and for this reason gardens have been easier to preserve.

233, 234 Two views of water in the
Topkapi gardens. Above: a pedestal fountain
set in a wide circular basin. Right: jets at the
edge of the peripheral terrace spray into a
pool adjacent to the Revan Kiosk
overlooking a section of the Topkapi Saray's
fourth court that was once a tulip garden.

216

THE ISLAMIC GARDEN AND COURTYARD TODAY

MOST GARDENS throughout the Islamic world were at one time accessible to and appreciated only by a privileged minority of rulers, courtiers and wealthy merchants. Courtyards, on the other hand, were available to almost everyone. All mosques and many dwellings, no matter how simple, possessed such a space. Together with the garden, the courtyard provided relief from the dust and clamour of the street, a degree of privacy and pleasure through water and planting, whether grand or humble.

Similar site, climatic, psychological and social considerations apply today. Escape from daily stress still remains desirable. Many needs such as strolling, sitting, the enjoyment of flowers and delight in water remain the same. Although advanced techniques in earth moving and sophisticated pumping mechanisms are now available, basic materials such as earth, planting, water and masonry are required. Enjoyment of all of a garden's elements – through the sense of sight, smell, touch and hearing – is still paramount. Yet some conditions have changed.

At first glance, Islamic gardens and courtyards seem to reflect a completeness and finality in their strict geometrical arrangement. In reality, the garden especially is inevitably in a state of transition, since it reflects the various generations who use it, the succession of gardeners who look after it and the living, natural materials with which it is composed. To some degree, therefore, there is a dichotomy in the Islamic garden, for despite the validity and strength of the original motivating idea, there is constant pressure for change, as well as continual risk of deterioration. Besides, the gardens of the Islamic world met particular requirements at particular epochs, and thus in a sense cannot be expected to last for all time.

The desires of society have also evolved. Originally, many Islamic gardens, through their size or relationship to particular buildings, expressed the power and prestige or benevolence of their founder. Today, these gardens no longer fulfil such a purpose, and subsequently perform a new role as a source of pleasure to the general public. Visited by many garden lovers, and providing a site for the celebration of festivals and holidays, the gardens now receive families from the city, parties of school-children, students with their books and young couples taking each other's photographs.

The original Islamic garden in its simplicity of conception and absence of elaborate detail, with its small number of users and large number of gardeners and assistants, was doubtless easy to maintain; and the upkeep of courtyards was likewise relatively effortless. In today's large gardens, an institution or branch of the government is usually the owner; and although this situation could ensure a measure of preservation and maintenance, the Islamic garden remains threatened in a number of ways.

235 Once a Mughal garden became a setting for the burial place of its owner, it was open to the public, and most of them remain to this day. Here families enjoy the quiet and shade of trees in the garden of the Tomb of Itimad-ud-Daula, Agra.

Some gardens, especially in Iran, are in earthquake zones, the destruction of Tabas providing a relatively recent example. A more prevalent threat is the economic one. Many gardens were once located on the fringe of a settlement; today, city growth has often increased the value of land to the point where an urban garden would be difficult to justify. In addition, not only has the expansion of traffic brought road widening, which has encroached on the edge of many gardens, but it has entailed the creation, in some cases, of new roads across existing gardens. The demand for increased food production has also placed great pressure on any easily accessible fertile land suitable for cultivation.

236 The interior of a pavilion adjacent to the source of the water that flows through the Bagh-i Fin near Kashan. Since the time of Shah Abbas, this paradise garden set at the edge of the desert has suffered from long periods of neglect. A little repair has recently been undertaken, but its drama and potential beauty deserve much greater attention.

237 An oratory in the Royal House at Medina Azahara near Cordova. In the courtyard is an ablution basin. The once luxurious gardens of this Umayyad caliphate have been desolate for centuries, but a limited restoration programme has been begun.

238 The remains of an early Islamic garden at Shahvanak, Shalvar Jig, near Tabriz. Although it is almost completely in ruins, the stone-edged pool still holds water, and there is a trace of a channel. Despite its condition, the location of this garden, set near a village amidst fields, retains something of its old charm.

Such pressure on garden land is a continuing threat. In recent years, a stadium has been built over the Bagh-i Shimal, Tabriz, and housing has been constructed on the site of the grand Bagh-i Takht, Shiraz. Near Granada, the upkeep of Velez Benaudalla has been found to be economically unfeasible; its unique asymmetrical design is still discernible and its dramatic hillside location is unaffected, but the garden is in ruins and overgrown. The Shalamar Bagh at Delhi has virtually disappeared, and part of the site of the Red Fort is used as a military garrison. In Kashmir, a new road has truncated Shalamar Bagh and,

239 The structures of Pari Mahal in Kashmir are in disrepair and some, such as this flanking pavilion, completely ruined. This condition is all the more unfortunate, since the planting is well cared for, and the views from it across the countryside are outstandingly beautiful.

unfortunately, Nishat Bagh, Pari Mahal and Hari Parbat are partly in ruins.

Even when not actually derelict, the condition of many gardens and courtyards remains far from ideal. A state of neglect and continual disrepair seems to be the fate of several. Meandering pipes, casual piles of brick, sand and broken stone carry a sad air of permanency. Many public gardens, especially in Iran, flaunt brightly coloured plastic garbage containers, crude light fixtures, piles of refuse, overhead wires loosely strung and vistas terminated by crumbling walls, tarpaulins or rough fencing. Formerly

240 The remains of a shallow, fluted fountain basin connected by channel to a deep rectangular tank at Chellah, Rabat. Plate 230 shows the whole courtyard in which this basin is located.

attractive courtyards, providing light and air to the bazaars they flank, have fared no better and are often choked with packing crates. Not only do such situations offend aesthetic sensibilities and impose limitations on photography, but more significantly, they reflect a general insensitivity on the part of administration and public to a potential source of beauty and benefit. Even when restoration work is commenced, it seems to be carried out inordinately slowly; many buildings are under scaffolding and many gardens contain ungainly heaps of building materials over a period of several years.

The absence of water in a courtyard or garden that was designed for it unfortunately detracts significantly from its enjoyment. The runnels in the gardens surrounding the tombs of Humayun in Delhi and Akbar in Sikandra have long been dry. More recently, the spring that once emerged within the upper pavilion of Chashma Shahi near Srinagar has been diverted to serve a newly constructed government building near by; as a result, the garden's water chute, channels and pools are now empty. Naturally, the diversion of a garden's water supply to irrigate surrounding fields may well be justified; happily, in the majority of cases, such diversion need be only partial or intermittent.

Restoration, unfortunately, has not often been considered a matter for exact scholarship, but, rather, a challenge to local creative abilities. Some gardens have been badly reconstructed as a result of misplaced 'interpretation'; planting has been inappropriate, and the original spirit of the garden has been seriously damaged.

Change continues. The Islamic garden has to be carefully observed, and those elements abstracted that are eternal. Although expressed in an earlier vocabulary, the unity and simplicity of the Islamic garden and courtyard still express much that is of significance for our own time.

241 A small domestic courtyard in
Cordova, the centre emphasized by the basin
in its star-shaped recess, and the usual semi-
tropical plants in pots.

242 A fountain basin in a courtyard of the
Hotel Transatlantique at Meknès. This is a
modern building consciously following
Islamic tradition, though without
pedantically copying particular models.

243 Another Cordova
courtyard, larger in scale,
with the characteristic
arches of Islam.

POSTSCRIPT

THE EARLY GARDEN was usually linked to a residence, and contained fruit trees and vegetables. The character of the garden rested on horticultural principles, specifically the species of plants and their arrangement, and this in turn depended on exposure to the sun and the availability of water. The design thus depended on irrigation, and was often based on simple geometry. Principally, the garden was watered from canals, and eventually this use of water led to an increase in the garden's range of design components. Pools were created, and then pavilions from which to enjoy them; and walls were built for the garden's overall protection. Many early garden concepts were also related to religious practices and the concept of a terrestrial paradise. For the wealthy and powerful, parks for hunting and wooded groves surrounded their palaces, and rich carpets, depicting gardens, graced the interior of their dwellings in winter.

It was in fact left largely to the cultured and prosperous to enjoy the concept of a garden designed for pleasure. In the Islamic world, the garden was often a scene for ceremonial, but it was also enjoyed in a relaxed, simple and natural manner, so clearly illustrated in numerous Iranian and Mughal miniatures.

The geometrical garden of the Western world mirrored the triumphs of man's reason over nature, while the romantic landscape garden echoed the human spirit's surrender to nature; in contrast, the Islamic garden reflected a balance of both approaches, the rational and the spiritual. Remarkably, this concept covered a time span of over a thousand years, and from west to east over the entire Islamic world. The same unity of spirit, for example, links the courtyards of the 14th-century Alhambra in Granada to the garden of the 17th-century Taj Mahal in Agra. Both garden and courtyard, whether in southern Spain under the Moors or in northwest India under the Mughals, had the same sense of affinity to the teachings of the Quran, the same spirit of serenity, the same awareness of outdoor space, the same ordered approach to layout, the same recognition of the natural qualities of plants and the same focus on water.

An early Muslim achievement was an image of paradise. This was consequently elaborated, and image became fused with reality. Behind this creation of every garden and courtyard was a standard of perfection. This is an ideal which has always remained the supreme motivation of the creative artist. Today in the Western world, art has become separated from both science and craftsmanship. Originally there was no schism. Art was once regarded as a science, and the striving for beauty, so evident in Islamic culture, was a part of the material world, and acknowledged by everyone from prince to tradesman. Only in our own day is the concept of beauty questioned. Standards of attractiveness, grace, charm and refinement are regarded as subjective, if indeed they are considered at all; whereas, it is ugliness that is recognized as a constituent of the real world. Design and execution are also today considered to be very different processes. The result of such attitudes is extremely unfortunate, since it is the degree to which beauty is related intrinsically to the very nature of things by which the values of a people, or a culture, or a civilization will eventually be judged.

PROPOSALS FOR RESTORATION AND PRESERVATION

IN ORDER TO ENSURE that an Islamic garden is correctly preserved, well maintained and fully appreciated, a number of steps may be taken. Initially, a comprehensive survey should be available of each existing garden as well as of possible garden sites. Existing conditions should be classified, based on an assessed degree of authenticity. Immediate steps for preservation should then be taken if there is any danger of encroachment, and, for this, legal powers such as zoning and acquisition would be necessary, with adequate administrative support.

There should be familiarity with the original design of architectural elements, such as pavilions, channels, fountains and paving, as well as of plant material, and its suitability. If a garden's early layout seems to have disappeared, traces of the original canal and pools as well as foundations of early buildings, walls, gateways and pavilions should be sought. The careful investigative restoration work undertaken in connection with the Bagh-i Babur at Kabul exemplifies this method. Sometimes a complete reconstruction involving the supply and containment of water, and the planting of trees, as well as the demolition of incongruous additions may be necessary to recreate an image of the garden's former splendour.

In financial terms, restoration and conservation may be encouraged by tax concessions, grants or long term loans; if a tourist attraction were to result, the initial outlay would provide its own economic justification. Professional and technical advice should be easily available, and provision could then be made for regular inspection. All such measures would be strengthened if they were to form part of an overall planning, restoration and conservation programme.

Restoration and conservation need a sense of art and history as well as technical ability. Achievement in these areas would no doubt be greater with the encouragement of public awareness and interest in the local and national cultural heritage. However, even though many gardens are today popularly enjoyed, their upkeep should not be regarded solely as a responsibility of government. It may be that new relationships between public and private sectors are required and these could possibly entail the formation of new institutions. Professional societies such as those of architecture and landscape architecture could well be involved.

There would seem to be ample justification for such concerted approaches. Constant change and loss of tradition is less attractive to most people than stability, and some measure of permanence and continuity with the past, together with the appreciation of a cultural heritage, remains highly desirable. In fact, many gardens and courtyards, although of varying authenticity, are already recognized to be of national importance, and are subsequently maintained by governments to varying degrees.

HORTICULTURAL NOTE

THIS BRIEF HORTICULTURAL NOTE lists popular names of some of the more common plants that are found in gardens throughout Islam. The list is inevitably limited, for, although it is true that some excellent records exist, there are not many and their accuracy cannot be entirely trusted. In addition, today's equivalents of some terms are not always known, and may suffer in translation. It is important to remember the obvious restrictions of soil conditions and climate; some plants are found in only certain parts of the world, while others, such as the rose and lilac, are found almost everywhere.

Trees Many trees are grown primarily for shade: cypress, elm, fir, maple, oak, pine, plane and spruce. Chenar, maple and spruce are colourful as well; the magnolia, in addition, is fragrant. Cypress, poplar and spruce take the form of sentinels, and are often planted in rows along paths, bordering a garden or leading to a focal point. Banana and coconut trees, date palms and olives have the additional attraction of providing food.

Shrubs Such shrubs as almond and quince bear fruit; together with lilac, they are also fragrant, while their flowers make splashes of colour. Myrtle is another popular fragrant shrub. Most shrubs in the Islamic garden are used as edging; box and hawthorn can be precisely trimmed, echoing the geometric character of the garden, and the latter is colourful, too, when in blossom.

Flowers Herbaceous plants are scattered at random in the grass or used as edging: anemone, bluebell, Bougainvillaea, hibiscus, larkspur, marigold, tulip, violet and wallflower. The carnation, daffodil, delphinium, jonquil, lily and rose are appreciated for their fragrance, which is also the prime attraction of the hyacinth and jasmine. Some plants have medicinal value; mint, saffron, sage and sweet marjoram are used for seasoning, and poppy seeds are edible too. Hollyhock and iris provide vertical accents as well as colour, and can be an interesting contrast with low massed cyclamen and lilies of the valley. Grass and moss are the chief forms of ground cover. Unique—in a class of its own— is the lotus, floating on the water of a still pool, which reflects its shape and colour.

Fruit The Islamic garden also contains fruit: fig, guava, lemon, lime, mandarin, mango, mulberry, pear and pomegranate. Most fruit tree blossoms, orange and peach particularly, provide colour, while apricot, cherry and plum are especially fragrant. Grape vines create shade if allowed to climb. Small trees such as hazelnut, pistachio, walnut and almond, which has beautiful pink and white blossom, produce a variety of delicious nuts.

Kitchen garden The kitchen garden is often an integral part of the Islamic garden. Artichoke, cabbage, eggplant, marrow (zucchini), pepper and pimento are popular vegetables; sugar cane is found also.

Trees, flowers, fruit, vegetables—the Islamic garden abounds with all, and for centuries the criteria for their selection have been shade, colour, fragrance and taste, criteria equally applicable when choosing plants for today's gardens and courtyards.

GLOSSARY

azulejos	tiles, predominantly blue
bagh	garden
bustan	(bostan) kitchen garden, orchard, garden
caravanserai	road guest-house, located on a trade route, for travellers and merchants with their goods
carmen	house and garden
causeway	raised stone pathway leading to a main structure, often with a water channel
chabutra	stone or marble platform on which the Emperor would sit, with water flowing around and beneath it
chadar	literally 'shawl'; stone or marble water chute, usually textured
char bagh	a term given to four gardens, or a garden divided into quadrants by water channels, as well as to a large garden containing a palace or pavilion
chenar	oriental plane tree
chini-kana	carved recess or niche behind a waterfall, to hold flowers or candles
courtyard	square or rectangular space bounded by walls or a building
Dar-al-Islam	territory ruled by the law of Islam
Diwan-i-Am	public audience hall
Diwan-i-Khas	private audience hall
glorieta	literally, 'little paradise', round pavilion or bower, symbolizing heaven
gul	rose; flower
gulistan	flower garden
hammam	bathing place; steam bath
huerta	orchard
inlay	specially cut pieces of semi-precious stone laid in sockets in stone or marble
Islam	literally 'surrender', from 'he who surrenders himself to the Divine Will gains peace'
iwan	(eyvan, ivan, or liwan) high entrance portal or vaulted recess with three sides enclosed
jali	perforated stone or marble window; lattice
khan	ruler, king
Khas Mahal	private palace
kiosk	open summer house or pavilion with roof on columns
Kufic	angular style of Arabic calligraphy, after town of Kufah, in Iraq
Maghrib	north-west Africa
mahal	house, palace in Mughal India

masjid	mosque, place of prostration, Islamic place of worship
mausoleum	burial place for royal person or other notable
medersa	(madrassa) theological seminary and educational building for orthodox Islamic studies
mihrab	niche in prayer wall of a building used for religious purposes, indicating the direction of Mecca, and thus of prayer
minaret	(minar) turret of mosque from which the call to prayer would be made
minbar	pulpit of a mosque
Moor	North African convert to Islam of Arab or Berber stock
muqarna	stalactite or honeycomb vault
musalla	place for prayer, often marked by divisions on the floor of a mosque within which prayer would be offered in prescribed postures
Muslim	(Moslem) adherent of Islam
naranjo	orange tree
Nashki	fluid style of Arabic calligraphy
patio	courtyard, usually within a dwelling, open to the sky
pavilion	ornamental building or open summer house, its roof often supported on columns
pietra-dura	see 'inlay'
qanat	underground canal
Quran	(Koran) sacred collection of Mohammed's work written in Arabic
reja	iron grille
riadh	(riyad) formal garden enclosed on two sides
sahn	interior central court of a mosque
shadirran	literally 'weir'; part of a fountain
Shah	title given the King of Iran
zenana	area of residence in which women in India were secluded (part of garden devoted to that purpose)
ziyada	outer court of a mosque

ISLAMIC DYNASTIES

Abbasids	caliphs of Baghdad, mid-8th to mid-13th centuries
Almohads	Berber dynasty in North Africa and Spain, 12th to 13th centuries, originating in the High Atlas
Almoravides	Berber dynasty in North Africa and Spain, mid-11th to mid-12th centuries, originating as nomads in the Sahara
Fatimids	rulers in Egypt, North Africa and Sicily, mid-10th to late 12th centuries
Mamluks	dynasty descending from Turkish slaves, which controlled Egypt and Syria from mid-13th to late 15th centuries
Marinids	dynasty in North Africa from mid-13th to mid-16th centuries
Mongols	invaded north-east Iran and desolated it in 13th century; based first in Tabriz and later in Sultaniya (also known in Iran as Ilkhanids)
Mughals	branch of the Timurids and founders of an empire based in Delhi and Agra, 16th to 19th centuries
Nasrids	local dynasty in Spain, 13th to 15th centuries
Ottomans	branch of Turks that founded an empire based in Istanbul, ruling in Turkey and Asia Minor from the early 14th century until after World War I
Saadians	dynasty in North Africa from mid-16th to mid-17th centuries
Safavids	dynasty in Iran from the start of 16th until mid-18th century
Samanids	dynasty in the region of Bokhara and Samarkand 9th to early 11th centuries
Sassanids	ruling dynasty of Iran prior to Muslim conquest
Seljuks	branch of Turks that ruled Iran and adjacent areas from mid-11th to end of 12th century; also in Anatolia until 13th century
Timurids	dynasty ruling from Samarkand and then Herat from late 14th until beginning of 16th century
Tulunids	dynasty in latter half of 9th century, based in Cairo
Umayyads	first caliphate from mid-7th until mid-8th century, with the capital at Damascus
Umayyads of Spain	8th- to 11th-century dynasty based in Cordova

MUGHAL EMPERORS 16th to 18th centuries

Akbar	'the great one', Great Mughal of India, mid-16th until beginning of 17th century
Aurangzeb	a Muslim purist and last of the great Mughal Emperors, from mid-17th to beginning of 18th century
Babur	'the tiger', first Mughal Emperor during first half of 16th century, in Samarkand and Kabul, before arriving in India
Humayun	second Mughal Emperor during mid-16th century, who spent much of his reign in exile in Iran, before finally returning to India
Jahangir	'world holder', Mughal Emperor at beginning of 17th century; his Persian wife, Nur Jahan, exerted great influence
Shah Jahan	'king of the world', fifth Mughal Emperor during mid-17th century; his Persian wife, Mumtaz Mahal, was also influential

	MOORISH SPAIN	SAFAVID IRAN	MUGHAL INDIA	OTHER REGIONS
622				Mohammed's flight to Mecca from Medina
800	Great Mosque, Cordova, 785–987			Great Mosque, Susa, 850–51 Karaouyne Mosque, Fez, 857 Ibn Tulun Mosque, Cairo, 876–79 Great Mosque, Qairawan (and successive centuries)
900	Medina Azahara, Cordova, 936–81 Alcazar, Cordova 950 Patio de los Naranjos, Seville, 976			al-Azhar Mosque, Cairo, 970–72
1000	Moorish Bath, Granada	Masjid-i Jami, Isfahan (Seljuk, 11th and 12th C., and successive centuries)		Qala of the Bani Hammad
1100	Great Mosque, Seville, 1172–82			San Giovanni degli Eremiti, Palermo, 1130 Aguedal, Marrakesh Menara Gardens, Marrakesh Cloisters, Monreale Cathedral, near Palermo, 1166–72
1200	Generalife, Granada, 1250 (or 1319)			
1300	Alhambra, Granada 1232–1408 (Patio de los Leones, 1377)	Masjid-i Jami, Kerman, 1349		Chellah, Rabat, 1310–39 Sahrij Medersa, Fez, 1322 Attarine Medersa, Fez, 1323–25 Bou Inaniye Medersa, Fez, 1350–55 Sultan Hassan Mosque, Cairo, 1356–63
1400	Casa de Pilatos, Seville, 1480–1571			Tomb of Tamerlane, Samarkand, 1402–34 Topkapi Saray, Istanbul (and successive centuries)
1500	Casa de los Tiros, Granada, 1505 Convent de Sta Catalina de Zafra, Granada, 1520–40	Nematollah Valli Shrine, Mahan, 16th and 17th C. Bagh-i Fin, Kashan (est. 16th C., present work early 19th century)	Ram Bagh, Agra, 1526 Naseem Bagh, Kashmir The Fort, Agra, 1564–80 Tomb of Humayun, Delhi, 1565–72 The Fort, Lahore, 1566 Fatehpur Sikri, 1569–80 Jahangiri Mahal, Agra, 1585 Hari Parbat, Kashmir, 1597	Medersa Ibn Youssef, Marrakesh (rebuilt 1565) Tombs of the Saadian Rulers, Marrakesh Mosque of Suleiman, Istanbul, 1556
1600		Maydan, Isfahan, 1597–1617 Ali Qapu, Isfahan (renovated 1598–1612) Masjid-i Shah Mosque, Isfahan, 1611–38 Char Bagh Avenue, Isfahan Chehel Sutun, Isfahan, 1647 (possibly earlier)	Tomb of Akbar, Sikandra, 1605–15 Verinagh, Kashmir, 1609 Shalamar Bagh, Kashmir, 1619 Tomb of Itimad-ud-Daula, Agra, 1622–28 Achabal, Kashmir Nishat Bagh, Kashmir, 1625 Lake Palace, Udaipur Pari Mahal, Kashmir Taj Mahal, Agra, 1630–53 Chashma Shahi, Kashmir, 1632 Tomb of Jahangir, Lahore, 1637 Red Fort, Delhi, 1639–48 Char Chenar Island, Kashmir Shalamar Bagh, Lahore, 1643 Jami Masjid, Delhi, 1644–58 Moti Masjid (Agra Fort), 1646–54 Pinjore, 1670	Oudaia Palace, Rabat Mamounia Gardens, Marrakesh
1700		Shah Goli, Tabriz (Qajar, possibly earlier) Mader-i Shah Medersa, Isfahan 1706–14 Chehel Tan, Shiraz, c. late 18th C. Haft Tan, Shiraz, c. late 18th C. Bagh-i Delgosha, Shiraz		
1800		Bagh-i Eram, Shiraz (possibly earlier) Bagh-i Gulshan, Shiraz 1863 Masjid-i Sepahsahar, Teheran 1878–90 Shah Zadeh Huseyn Shrine, Qasvin Narenjestan-i Qavam, Shiraz Gulistan Palace, Teheran, late 18th C., early 19th C.		Dar Jamai Palace, Meknès Bahia Palace, Marrakesh, 1894–1900

Select Chronology of Gardens and Courtyards
Note: In many instances, dates are approximate

SELECT BIBLIOGRAPHY

Moorish Spain Byne, M. S. and A. *Spanish Gardens and Patios* (London, J. B.Lippincott Co. 1928)
Dickie, James 'The Hispano-Arab Garden. Its Philosophy and Function' in *Bulletin, School of Oriental Studies, London University*, vol. xxxi (1968), pp. 237–48
Nichols, R. S. *Spanish and Portuguese Gardens* (New York, Houghton Mifflin Co. 1924)
Prieto-Moreno, Francisco *Los Jardines de Granada* (Madrid, Direccion General de Bellas Artes 1973)
Sordo, E. *Moorish Spain* (London, Elek Books 1963)
Villiers-Stuart, C. M. *Spanish Gardens* (London, B. T. Batsford Ltd 1929)

Safavid Iran Arberry, A. J. ed. *Legacy of Persia* (Oxford, Clarendon Press, 1953)
Ardalan, Nader and Bakhtiar, Laleh *The Sense of Unity* (Chicago, University of Chicago Press 1973)
Chardin, Sir John *The Travels of Sir John Chardin in Persia*, tr. E. Lloyd (London, Argonaut Press 1927)
Hanway, Jonas *British Trade over the Caspian Sea* (London, Osborne and Brown 1754)
Isfahan City of Light: Exhibition organized by Ministry of Culture and Arts of Iran (Teheran 1976)
Pope, Arthur Upham *Introducing Persian Architecture* (London, Oxford University Press 1969)
——*A Survey of Persian Art from Prehistoric Times to the Present* (London, Oxford University Press 1964)
Wilber, Donald N. *Persian Gardens and Garden Pavilions* (Rutland, Vermont, Charles E. Tuttle Co. 1962)

Mughal India Abu-i Fay'l ibn Murbarack *The Akbar Nama*, tr. H. Beveridge (Bengal, Asiatic Society of Bengal 1935)
Babur, *Babur-Nama (Memoirs of Babur)*, tr. A. S. Beveridge (New Delhi, Oriental Books Reprint Corp. 1970)
Crowe, Sylvia and Haywood, Sheila *The Gardens of Mughul India* (London, Thames and Hudson 1972)
Gascoigne, Bamber *The Great Moghuls* (London, Jonathan Cape 1973)
Hambly, G. *Cities of Mughal India* (London, Elek Books Ltd 1968)
Jahangir, *Tuzuk-i-Jahangiri or Memoirs of Jahangir*, tr. A. Rogers, ed. H. Beveridge (London 1968)
Jairzbhoy, R. A. 'Early Garden Palaces of the Great Mughals' in *Oriental Art* IV (1958), pp. 68–75
Khan, Muhammad Wali Ullah *Lahore and its Monuments* (Karachi, Department of Archaeology and Museums, Ministry of Education 1973)
Nath, R. *Marg*, vol. XXVI, no. 1, December (1972)
Sanwal, B. D. *Agra and its Monuments* (New Delhi, Orient Longmans 1968)
Schweitzer, C. 'Muslim Waterworks' in *Islamic Culture* XIII (1939), pp. 79–82
Sharma, Y. D. *Delhi and its Neighbourhood* (New Delhi, Archaeological Survey of India 1974)
Villiers-Stuart, C. M. *Gardens of the Great Mughals* (London, A. and C. Black 1913)
—— 'Indian Water Gardens' in *Journal of the Royal Society of Arts* vol. LXII, 10 April (1914), pp. 447–64

Volwahsen, Andreas *Living Architecture: Islamic Indian* (New York, Grosset and Dunlap 1970)

Other regions Davis, F. *The Palace of Topkapi in Istanbul* (New York, Charles Scribner's Sons 1970)

de Clavijo, R. G. *Narrative of the Embassy of Ruy Gonzalez de Clavijo to the Court of Timur at Samarkand 1403–6*, tr. C. R. Markham (London, Hakluyt Society Papers 1870)

Gallotti, Jean *Le Jardin et la Maison Arabe au Maroc* (Paris, Editions Albert Levy 1926)

Hill, Derek *Islamic Architecture in North Africa* (London, Faber and Faber 1976)

Landau, R. *Morocco* (London, Elek Books Ltd, 1967)

Marçais, Georges *Melanges d'Histoire et d'Archeologie de l'Occident musulman* (Algiers 1957)

Parpagliolo, M. T. S. *Kabul: The Bagh-i Babur* (Rome, Istituto Italiano per il Medio e l'Estremo Oriente 1972)

World of Islam Burckhardt, Titus *Art of Islam: Language and Meaning* (London, World of Islam Festival Publishing Co. Ltd 1976)

The Encyclopaedia of Islam (Leiden, E. J. Brill 1960)

Encyclopaedia of World Art, vol. viii (New York, McGraw Hill 1959)

Hoag, John D. *Islamic Architecture* (New York, Harry N. Abrams Inc. 1977)

Islamic Gardens: Proceedings, 2nd International Symposium on Protection and Restoration of Historical Gardens (Paris, International Council of Monuments and Sites 1976)

Lewis, Bernard ed. *The World of Islam* (London, Thames and Hudson 1976)

MacDougall, E. and Ettinghausen, R. eds *The Islamic Garden* (Washington D.C., Dumbarton Oaks Trustees for Harvard University 1976)

Mundy, Peter *Travels of Peter Mundy in Europe and Asia 1608–67* (London, Hakluyt Society Papers 1906–37)

Scerrato, Umberto *Monuments of Civilisation: Islam* (New York, Grosset and Dunlap 1976)

Speiser, Werner *Oriental Architecture in Colour* (London, Thames and Hudson 1965)

Toynbee, Arnold ed. *Cities of Destiny* (London, Thames and Hudson, 1967)

Landscape architecture Berrall, Julia S. *The Garden: an Illustrated History* (London, Thames and Hudson 1966)

Hyams, Edward *A History of Gardens and Gardening* (London, J. M. Dent 1971)

Jellicoe, Susan and Geoffrey *The Landscape of Man* (London, Thames and Hudson 1975)

———*Water: The Use of Water in Landscape Architecture* (London, A. and C. Black 1971)

Kassler, Elizabeth B. 'Water and Architecture' in *Architectural Record*, vol. 123, June (1958), pp. 137–52

———'Why Water' in *Architectural Record*, vol. 124, May (1959), pp. 189–96

———'Water Inside and Out' in *Architectural Record*, vol. 124, June (1959), pp. 165–74

Newton, Norman T. *Design on the Land* (Cambridge, The Belknap Press of Harvard University Press 1976)

AUTHOR'S ACKNOWLEDGMENTS

Acknowledgment is made to the Canada Council, whose research grant to assess the role of decoration in Islamic and contemporary architecture first provided an introduction to the heritage of Uzbekistan, Iran, India and Pakistan; to the Shastri Indo-Canadian Institute, whose award of a Senior Fellowship generously provided the time and opportunity to study the role of gardens and water in Mughal architecture; to the University of Manitoba's Research Board for assistance towards the purchase of sketching material, film, and the cost of drafting; to Bruce R. Rasmussen for his drafting skills; and to all at Thames and Hudson.

Many people assisted overseas, particularly Mrs G. S. Karnouk of the American University in Cairo, Miss F. Z. Mataoui of the Bardo Museum in Algiers, and Mr H. Rabanyar and Mr S. J. Toorobi of Tabriz.

Lisa Golombek, Ian Kerr, Edward C. Moulton and Louise Sweet willingly read the manuscript and contributed many helpful comments; shortcomings remain the responsibility of the author.

Sources of the quotations

Setting the scene   D. N. Wilber's contemporary description of the Persian garden from his *Persian Gardens and Garden Pavilions*

Characteristics   Babur's Description of a stream in Kabul from *Babur-Nama (Memoirs of Babur)*, tr. A. S. Beveridge

Safavid Iran   Chardin's description of the Iranian garden and of standing enjoyment from *The Travels of Sir John Chardin in Persia*
Description of a garden at Khoi from J. Morier *A Journey through Persia, Armenia and Asia Minor* quoted in Arthur Upham Pope *A Survey of Persian Art from Prehistoric Times to the Present*
T. Herbert's description of Isfahan and of swinging in the trees from his *Some yeares travels into Africa and Asia* quoted in Arthur Upham Pope *A Survey of Persian Art from Prehistoric Times to the Present*
Description of narcissus meadows from *The geographical part of the Nuzhat al-Qulub composed by Hamd Mustawfi, 1346*, tr. Le Strange, quoted in Arthur Upham Pope *A Survey of Persian Art from Prehistoric Times to the Present*

Mughal India   Description of Kashmir from *Tuzuk-i-Jahangiri* or *Memoirs of Jahangir*, tr. A. Rogers, ed. H. Beveridge
Account of Babur's first garden in Agra from *Babur-Nama (Memoirs of Babur)*, tr. A. S. Beveridge
F. Bernier's account of a *chini-kana* from his *Collections of Travels through Turkey into Persian and the East Indies* quoted in S. Crowe and S. Haywood *The Gardens of Mughal India*

235

Other regions   Ibn Jubayr's description of Damascus quoted in N. A. Ziadeh *Damascus under the Mamluks*
Clavijo's description of gardens in Samarkand quoted in E. Hymas *A History of Gardens and Gardening*
Babur's description of Kabul quoted in D. N. Wilber *Persian Gardens and Garden Pavilions*
Babur's description of the Bagh-i Wafa from *Babur-Nama (Memoirs of Babur)*, tr. A. S. Beveridge

Sources of the plans

All plans have been specially drawn for this book, and are based mainly but not exclusively on the following sources:

Setting the scene   Scerrato, U. *Monuments of Civilisation: Islam* Bibi Khanum Mosque, Samarkand
Wilber, D. N. *Persian Gardens and Garden Pavilions* Hasht Behesht, Isfahan

Moorish Spain   Byne, M. S. and A. *Spanish Gardens and Patios* Alcazar, Seville
Prieto-Moreno, F. *Los Jardines de Granada* Generalife, Granada; Palacio de Daralhorra, Granada; Velez Benaudalla, near Granada
Sordo, E. *Moorish Spain* Alhambra, Granada; Patios de los Naranjas, Cordova

Safavid Iran   Ardalan, N. and Bakhtiar, L.. *The Sense of Unity* Bazaar (segment), Kashan; General Plan, Isfahan
Burckhardt, T. *Art of Islam: Language and Meaning* Masjid-i Shah, Isfahan
Isfahan City of Light Mader-i Shah Madersa, Isfahan; Masjid-i Jami, Isfahan
Pope, A. U., *Introducing Persian Architecture* Narenjestan-i Qavam, Shiraz
Wilber, D. N. *Persian Gardens and Garden Pavilions* Bagh-i Eram, Shiraz; Bagh-i Fin, Kashan; Bagh-i Gulshan, Shiraz; Chehel Sutun, Isfahan; Fathabad, near Tabriz; Haft Tan, Shiraz; Shah Goli, Tabriz

Mughal India   Crowe, S. and Haywood, S. *The Gardens of Mughal India* Achabal, Kashmir; Chashma Shahi, Kashmir; The Fort (Anguri Bagh), Agra; Nishat Bagh, Kashmir
Hoag, J. D., *Islamic Architecture* The Fort (Pearl Mosque), Agra; Red Fort, Delhi; Tomb of Jahangir, Lahore
Kassler, E. B. *Architectural Record* (June 1959) Red Fort (private apartments), Delhi
Khan, M. W. U. *Lahore and its Monuments* The Fort, Lahore
Sanwal, B. D. *Agra and its Monuments* The Fort, Agra; Ram Bagh, Agra; Tomb of Akbar, Sikandra; Tomb of Itimad-ud-Daula, Agra
Sharma, Y. D. *Delhi and its Neighbourhood* Red Fort, Delhi
Villiers-Stuart, C. M. *Gardens of the Great Mughals* Lake Palace, Udaipur; Shalamar Bagh, Kashmir; Shalamar Bagh, Lahore
Volwahsen, A. *Living Architecture: Islamic Indian* General Plan, Fatehpur Sikri; Taj Mahal, Agra; Tomb of Humayun, Delhi

Other regions   Burckhardt, T. *Art of Islam: Language and Meaning* Sultan Hassan Mosque, Cairo
Hoag, J. D. *Islamic Architecture* Attarine Medersa, Fez; Bou Inaniye Medersa, Fez; Bulkawara Palace, Samarra; Karaouyne Mosque, Fez
Speiser, W. *Oriental Architecture in Colour* Ibn Tulun Mosque, Cairo

INDEX

Numbers in *italic* refer to picture captions. Roman numerals are those of the colour plates.